The Facts
of Life

THE
F·A·C·TS
OF
L·I·F·E

*Science and the
Abortion Controversy*

Harold J. Morowitz
James S. Trefil

New York   Oxford
OXFORD UNIVERSITY PRESS
1992

Oxford University Press

Oxford   New York   Toronto
Delhi   Bombay   Calcutta   Madras   Karachi
Kuala Lumpur   Singapore   Hong Kong   Tokyo
Nairobi   Dar es Salaam   Cape Town
Melbourne   Auckland

and associated companies in
Berlin   Ibadan

Copyright © 1992 by Harold J. Morowitz and James S. Trefil

Published by Oxford University Press, Inc.,
200 Madison Avenue, New York, New York 10016

Oxford is a registered trademark of Oxford University Press

Library of Congress Cataloging-in-Publication Data
Morowitz, Harold J.
The facts of life : science and the abortion controversy / Harold
J. Morowitz and James S. Trefil.
p. cm.   Includes bibliographical references and index.
ISBN 0-19-507927-2
1. Embryology, Human.   2. Human reproduction.   3. Abortion.
I. Trefil, James S., 1938–   . II. Title.
[DNLM: 1. Abortion, Legal—United States.   2. Public Policy-
-United States.   3. Science.   WQ 440 M869f]
QM601.M768   1992
612.6'4—dc20   DNLM/DLC   92-16343

1 3 5 7 9 8 6 4 2

Printed in the United States of America
on acid-free paper

To George Johnson
and His Vision of the University

Preface

It is almost impossible to live in the United States today and be unaware of the heated and divisive debate that surrounds the abortion controversy. There are few subjects in the public arena that touch individuals more deeply, or that engender such strong emotions. In such an overheated atmosphere, it might seem that there is little that scientific inquiry could add. Sometimes it seems that rationality itself has been excluded. Nevertheless, we believe that significant new information has been brought to light in the last few decades — information that speaks directly to many of the arguments made by people on both sides of the issue.

If you've already made up your mind on the subject of abortion, this book probably won't change it, although it may add a depth of understanding to your position. If you haven't made up your mind, or if you have misgivings about the whole question, you will find information here that may help you come to firm conclusions. While no one is going to make a decision on abortion purely on scientific grounds, we feel that everyone, at the very least, ought to get the facts straight. To that end we explore the areas of science that bear on the abortion controversy, explaining what we know today that wasn't known when the whole subject blew up in the 1970s and why that knowledge is relevant to the debate.

The idea for this book arose in the late summer of 1991, when the nomination of Clarence Thomas to the Supreme Court made it seem likely that *Roe v. Wade* would be overturned and the country would be plunged, state by state, into an intense debate on abortion. One of us (HJM) began to think about writing a friend-of-the-court brief, laying out the best scientific knowledge available. Thanks to an innovative program at George Mason University, the authors have offices next to each other, although we are in different disciplines. Daily conversations and interactions made us realize that there was more to be said than could be contained in a short brief, and that what we were finding deserved a much wider readership.

The one overriding principle on which we agreed at the start was to make every effort to present the diverse science as accurately as possible. This meant that whenever possible we would visit or talk on the phone to people generally recognized as leaders in the different fields of research we were reporting, and at the very least that we would track down claims in the original research papers, rather than rely on secondary sources and reports. Sometimes this method led us to unexpected results. We found, for example (see page 122), that a bit of "common knowledge" used by people on all sides of the abortion controversy is simply wrong.

In the first seven chapters of this book, we present the results of a search through the sciences. This presentation is as dispassionate and objective as possible. In the final chapter, we discuss policy on the basis of the scientific findings. Here, obviously, our own opinions and sensibilities have to enter the picture, and we do not try to conceal the fact that they do. Finally, in the Afterword, we make individual statements about our feelings about the abortion issue so that the reader can judge the extent to which those feelings may have colored the earlier discussion.

During the course of writing this book, we have been fortunate enough to receive useful comments and help from many of our colleagues, friends, and relatives. With the usual caveat that we alone are responsible for any errors that may remain in the text, we wish to thank:

Gordon Avery, *George Washington University Medical School*

Mary Catherine Bateson, *George Mason University*

Michael Bennett, *Albert Einstein College of Medicine*

Charles Black, *Columbia University Law School*

Veronica Feeg, *George Mason University School of Nursing*

Penny Glass, *George Washington University Medical School*

Philip Gingerich, *University of Michigan Museum of Paleontology*

Gregory Holmes, *Children's Hospital, Boston*

Peter Hoppe, *Jackson Laboratory, Bar Harbor*

Patricia King, *Georgetown Law School*

Father Thomas King, *Georgetown University*

Joshua Lederberg, *Rockefeller University*

Frank Loew, *Tufts University Veterinary School*

Robert Macnab, *Yale University*

Eugenie Mielczarek, *George Mason University*

Joshua Morowitz, *New Britain Hospital*

John Paden, *George Mason University*

Bruce Palmer, *Maui Community College*

Rabbi James Ponet, *Yale University*

Pasko Rakic, *Yale University*
Kenneth Schaffner, *George Washington University Medical School*
Rebecca Simmons, *Children's Memorial Hospital, Chicago*
Abigail Smith, *Yale University School of Medicine*
B. Holly Smith, *University of Michigan Museum of Anthropology*
Temple Smith, *Boston University*
Davor Solter, *University of Freiberg*
Melissa Stanley, *George Mason University*
William Summers, *Yale University School of Medicine*
James K. Trefil, *University of Virginia Law School*
Ira Weiss, *George Washington University Medical School*
James Willett, *George Mason University*
James Wilson, *Yerkes Primate Center*
John W. Wilson, *George Mason University*

Fairfax, Virginia   H.J.M.
June 1992   J.S.T.

Contents

The Facts
of Life

I

Asking the Right Question

Ever since the *Roe v. Wade* decision of 1973, the debate over abortion has never been far from the center of American political and social consciousness. The recent hearing by the U.S. Supreme Court on Pennsylvania's abortion law means that the debate will become even more intense as every state legislature in the country grapples with the issue.

There are many facets to this debate—many different ways of approaching the issue. Whether abortion should be allowed can be (and has been) viewed as a legal, moral, social, political, and religious question. It clearly touches on all of these areas.

But there is another aspect to the abortion debate that has received very little attention. The biological sciences can provide a unique perspective on abortion. Most discussion of abortion, after all, focuses on the nature of the developing fetus and on whether it is a "person" worthy of being accorded legal protection. People may say, for example, that the fetus is capable of feeling pain at a certain stage of development, or is capable of thought, or simply looks like a human being. All of these kinds of arguments depend on comparing the fetus to full-term infants and then coming to some operational conclusion on the basis of that comparison.

Our approach is to look at both adult and fetus as a biologist would: as parts of a complex and interconnected web of living things on our planet. Instead of asking about how a fetus resembles an adult human, we propose to ask how both of them differ from other living things, what it is that makes them uniquely human, and then to use this information in coming to policy decisions. Over the years, scientists have developed new understandings about life on our planet and about the nature of *Homo sapiens*. A good deal of this understanding has come since the original *Roe* decision and, to our knowledge, has been largely ignored in the ensuing debate. It shouldn't be.

This is not to say that the abortion debate can be reduced, in the end, to a question of scientific fact. It can't. Neither, however, can the debate be conducted intelligently if one ignores what scientists have learned about human beings and about the process by which a single fertilized egg develops into a newborn child. This truth is nowhere more evident than when legislators trying to grapple with the abortion issue turn to the scientific community and ask, "When does an individual life begin?"

This is not only the wrong question, it is a question that cannot be answered by use of methods of science. Any scientist who says it can either doesn't understand the limits of our craft, has defined "life" in a way that he or she hasn't made explicit, or is trying to be deceptive. We've seen examples of all three sources of error behind "scientific" answers to this question, by people on both sides of the abortion debate.

This question is sometimes confused with one that is more specifically biological: "When does life in general begin?" meaning, "When did living things first appear on the earth?" This more general question can, of course, be approached with the methods of science, although the fact of the matter is that *life* is one of those terms (like *time*) that scientists are usually quite content to use in a loose, colloquial way, but that they find extraordinarily difficult to define with precision.

In the context of the abortion debate, *life* clearly means "the life of an individual." So "When does life begin?" is still the wrong question. The only way we can define *individual life* is by making a list of the characteristics of an individual life and then seeing if the entity in question shares them. The only rational answer a biologist can give to the question "When does an individual life begin?" is to say, "Tell me what you mean by *individual life*, and I'll tell you if this entity has it." A biologist, in other words, cannot provide a definition of *individual life* (at least as that term is used in the abortion debate) solely from the biological sciences. He or she must go outside science for these sorts of definitions. For example, a geneticist can tell you that at conception a new combination of preexisting DNA has come into existence, but whether "life" has begun simply cannot be resolved by this information. This type of answer is profoundly unsatisfying, but it's about all you can expect if you ask the wrong question.

This is not to say that biologists don't know a great deal about human beings and how they develop; indeed, one of the purposes of this book is to sift through the mass of information scientists have accumulated over the years and to extract material relevant to the abortion controversy. We approach abortion from the scientific point of view, and we must be very careful about drawing the line between what we know about the development of a fetus and use of terms that carry enormous emotional freight such as *life*, *person*, and even, in some cases, *human being*.

For our purposes, the most important fact about human beings (by which we mean members of the species *Homo sapiens*) that biologists have affirmed is: *Human beings are profoundly similar to all other forms of life, yet profoundly different.*

Let's take these statements one at a time. For most of recorded history, it was believed that human beings were in some way special—somehow different from other animals. Since Descartes, this idea has been cast in terms of a statement about humans having souls and animals being soulless.

Starting with Darwin in the mid-nineteenth century, however, biologists have come to realize that humans aren't as different from the animals as we might like to think. Scientists have found that human beings and lower animals share a common ancestry, and over the years have been able to trace that ancestry in the fossil record (see Chapter 4).

Over the last few decades, scientists have come to realize that there is an even more fundamental connection between human beings and other living things. At the most basic level—the level of most molecules inside our cells—human beings are functionally indistinguishable from other living things. Not only do human cells function in pretty much the same way as those of other animals, but they often use the very same molecules to carry out the same tasks. And this basic biochemical identity of humanity with the rest of life doesn't stop at animals. As we point out in Chapter 2, humans aren't all that different from plants and bacteria at the molecular level.

Given this profound connection of human beings to the rest of the living world, how can we explain the profound differences that set us apart? While it may be true that some apes and monkeys possess a rudimentary ability to learn languages and make tools, it's clear that an enormous gulf exists between us and them in these areas. Apes do not build cities (although they do have complex social structures), and more important, they do not build enduring cultures.

One problem with the question "When does life begin?" is that it concentrates our attention on the basic chemistry that we share with all other living things. It asks about the functioning of cells. So even if we could give it a scientific answer, the answer would say nothing about what it is that makes human beings different and special.

There is a great deal to be learned from reformulating the discussion of the abortion issue in terms of another question. We concentrate attention not on the properties we share with other animals, but on the properties that make us uniquely human. We do not ask "When does life begin?" but "When does the fetus acquire those properties that make humans uniquely different from other living things?"

We will use the somewhat cumbersome phrase "the acquisition of humanness" to describe the process by which the fetus develops its distinctly human traits, or by which human beings as a group evolved from more primitive ancestors. We use this emotionally neutral phrase to describe the process by which the human branch emerged from the evolutionary tree or by which an individual fetus becomes a member of our species. As we shall show, many of the standard terms that we might have used have legal, moral, or religious overtones that make them unsuitable for our purposes.

In our language, then, the relevant question is "When does a fetus (or embryo or zygote) acquire humanness?" Given our definition of humanness, this question can be answered totally within the framework of science. We first look at human beings and determine what property or properties distinguish them from other living things. Then, we examine the development of a human being from a single fertilized egg to birth and determine when those properties are acquired.

We should emphasize that at this point we make no presumption about when humanness is acquired. For example, it could turn out that humanness is associated with the coming together of the parental DNA in fertilization, in which case we would say that humanness is acquired at conception. It could just as easily turn out that the relevant properties are not present until birth, in which case we would say that a fetus never acquires the properties of humanness. Thus the question we are asking can, in principle, be answered by designating any specific time between conception and birth. In this sense, it is a neutral question.

It is also, however, a complex and difficult question. To answer it, we require an understanding of evolution and organismic biology (to find what separates humans from other animals), molecular biology (to understand in what ways they are the same), embryology (to understand what actually happens during pregnancy), neurophysiology (to understand the functioning of the human brain), and many other fields. No individual scientist can be expected to know everything that bears on the question of the acquisition of humanness; indeed, we have found that experts in one relevant discipline often don't talk much to those in another. During the course of writing this book, however, we have undertaken to read the current literature and contact a number of people, either by phone or in person, to help us develop the understanding we want to share with our readers.

Finally, we should point out that our question need not necessarily have a precise answer. We may not, for example, be able to come up with a statement like "The fetus acquires humanness on the 203rd day following conception." In fact, we have found that there are rather large gray areas. Sometimes, they are due to lack of sufficient research in particular domains. More often, however, the existence of gray areas is inherent in the nature of biological systems themselves. In these cases, we will be able only to define the borders of grayness and leave it to others to use methods outside the sciences to make decisions.

Why Asking the Right Question Is Important

If you follow the abortion debate for any length of time, you will hear statements made in the heat of political battle that tend to blur distinctions between concepts that should be kept separate. Worse, the choice of a word often prejudges the entire debate. This is one reason why we insist on talking about "the acquisition of humanness," as cumbersome as the phrase is. For example, if a speaker refers to abortion as "the slaughter of innocent children," or to antiabortionists as "murderers of women," there's obviously not much hope of a rational discussion. But even a seemingly innocuous reference to a "fetus" or a "person" can carry with it the entire burden of a political position. For this reason, we discuss here some terms that come up frequently in the debate.

Person

Personhood is a legal concept. In law, a *person* is defined as a legal entity recognized by law as having rights and duties. In terms of individuals, a person is someone who is entitled to specific legal protections, and *personhood* signifies the state of enjoying those protections.*

---

*The legal concept *personhood* need not apply only to individual people; it extends to entities like corporations and estates.

One of the most basic rights is the right to life, and the taking of a human life without the sanction of the state is considered one of the most serious of crimes. It is, in fact, called *murder*.

If the fetus is called a person, then, it follows automatically that the act of abortion is murder. By definition of the term, there can be no other conclusion. Thus, one important question in the legal debate over abortion revolves around whether the fetus is, in fact, a person in the legal sense.

The concept of personhood as applied to individuals is not the same from one society to the next. In modern Western cultures, for example, there is no debate whatsoever about the proposition that personhood is conferred on a child at birth; the argument is solely about whether personhood extends back all or part of the way to conception. But this definition of the newborn infant as a person is not universal around the world, nor has it been universally adopted throughout history.

In ancient Sparta, for example, leaving a child to die of exposure on a hillside was not considered an act of murder if that child was judged unsuitable for some reason. Thus, in Sparta personhood was conferred some time after birth. In the same way, female babies in rural China were once routinely killed—a practice that some believe persists to this day.

In regions of rural Japan, there was an interesting variation on this theme. Personhood was conferred on a baby when it uttered its first cry. If an attending midwife saw that the infant was unsuitable (by reason of its characteristics or for societal survival reasons) and it was allowed to die before it uttered its first cry, no murder was held to have taken place. In Jewish Talmudic law, on the other hand, a full-term baby acquires personhood as soon as the head emerges, but somewhat later if the baby is premature.

Because of the importance of the Judeo-Christian tradition in America, it is important to understand abortion as dealt with in the Old Testament. The most significant fact is that it is never mentioned. Given that most of the societies surrounding Israel banned abortion (some required the death penalty for it), the lack of any comment on the issue when the laws were written is itself significant. That the fetus was not considered a person *in utero* is attested to by this passage from the Book of Exodus (21:22)

> and if men strive together, and hurt a woman with child, so that there is a miscarriage, and yet no harm follows, the one who hurt her shall be fined, according as the woman's husband shall lay on him, and he shall pay as the judges determine.

Other examples:

- In Northern Ghana, it was common practice to wait until seven days after birth before regarding a child as human. Only then could people be sure that it was not a spirit child.
- Among native American tribes in the Mojave, a child who lived long enough to be put to the breast could no longer be killed.
- Among the Ayatal aborigines of Formosa, there was no punishment for killing a child before it was named (i.e., less than two or three years old).
- On the island of Truk, deformed infants were considered ghosts and were burned or thrown into the ocean. Trukese were horrified at the suggestion that this act was infanticide.

The point of these examples is that although the concept of personhood is very well defined, the point at which it is conferred on an individual depends on where and when that individual lives. In the context of the societies mentioned above, there is nothing morally wrong with killing children after birth; no murder is involved. Contemporary Westerners recoil from these acts in horror because we have a different set of values, values based on the conferring of personhood no later than birth. From a purely legal point of view, all of these various cultural systems are equivalent because each has a well-defined point at which a human being becomes a person.

Soul

Soul is a religious concept, closely related to the concept of *person.* If you believe that a soul exists, then the soul is what makes humans different from other living things. In our language, it is what defines humanness.

Although there is no necessary logical connection between someone's having a soul and being a person, in practice the two are very closely related in some modern thought. The presumption is that once an individual acquires a soul, he or she is fully a person and therefore entitled to legal protection.

The question of the existence of a soul is not a scientific one. There is no such thing as a "soul meter" that we can attach to an adult or fetal human being to detect the presence of a soul. The notion is preposterous on its face. Scientists can measure observables: the DNA content of a cell, the shape and weight of a particular organ. We cannot measure something that is, by definition, unmeasurable.

Like personhood, the concept of the presence or absence of a soul is different from one religious tradition to the next. In the Christian tradition, every human being has an eternal soul. During the Middle Ages a great deal of thought went into the question of when that soul was acquired—it was called the problem of "ensoulment." There was not, however, universal agreement on when ensoulment occurred, although it was generally agreed that it happened before birth. The basic idea was that the body had to be prepared to receive the soul, that there had to be something resembling a human being for ensoulment to occur. Based on reports of examinations of miscarried embryos, Thomas Aquinas taught that ensoulment occurred at forty days for the male embryo and at ninety days for the female. In difficult deliveries, when those in attendance felt that the child and the mother might both die, it was standard procedure to baptize the unborn baby; indeed, there is a special instrument, called a *baptismal syringe*, that was (and is) used for this purpose. Today, Catholic priests routinely baptize stillborn infants.

In many religions the concept of an eternal soul is not as clear as in Christianity. In the traditional Navaho religion, for example, a person's good aspects simply disappear at death, leaving behind his evil and weak parts to become a *chindi*, or evil spirit. In both the Hindu and Buddhist traditions, with their belief in reincarnation, the possession of something like a soul (*atman*) is not reserved for human beings. In fact, a given soul may be associated with many different life forms over time.

The idea that a human being receives an eternal soul sometime after conception is something that is very strong in the Christian tradition, but by no means universal among human societies.

Patient

Patient is a medical term and refers to the rights that someone has in a specific medical setting. For example, someone who comes into a hospital in the United States in distress cannot legally be turned away just because he or she cannot pay for services, no matter how expensive they may be. Other countries, less wealthy than the United States and with fewer medical facilities, do not grant the right of patienthood so freely. As with the terms *person* and *soul,* the conferring of patienthood varies from one culture to the next.

Human Being

In common usage, the term *human being* is often used as if it were synonymous with *person* or with *soul.* "Abortion is murder" and "Abortion kills human beings" are used as equivalent statements. This usage is unfortunate, because the term has a precise biological meaning. In biology, an entity is a human being if it is a member of the species *Homo sapiens.* In this sense, the term carries no legal or religious connotations. It is simply a statement that the organism meets certain anatomical and genetic criteria. For our purposes, we will say that a human being is someone who has recognizably human DNA. A more precise statement of what this means will be available when the Human Genome Project is completed.

In the precise language of the biological sciences, the correct way to refer to a fetus is as a developmental stage of the species *Homo sapiens.* In this context, one can say that a human being exists from conception on, but it does not follow that that human being is a person or has a soul.

Humanness

Humanness, of course, is the concept we introduced above, and it is defined as the possession of those properties that distinguish human beings from other living things. Like *human being, hu-*

manness is defined here in purely biological terms and thus cannot vary from one culture to the next. Like the term *human being*, *humanness* in and of itself carries no religious or moral connotations. The question of whether it is wrong to kill someone who has acquired humanness cannot be answered from within the tenets of science itself but has to be decided by some external criteria.

This is an extremely important point, so at the risk of belaboring the obvious we'll illustrate it with an example. Consider a child born in rural Japan in the sixteenth century. This child became a human being at conception and acquired humanness at some later (and as yet undefined) date. It acquired personhood (and legal protection) only after giving its first cry. In our language, it was possible in that particular society both to be a human being and to acquire humanness, but still not to be a person.

One other point about humanness should be made. We have chosen a reasonable biological definition for this term. Someone else may wish to use the term differently: one might want to say, "It has humanness if it looks human" or "It has humanness if it has human DNA." There is no reason why there can't be many alternate definitions of humanness. The point, however, is that the concept is morally neutral. Giving a definition of humanness and determining when it is acquired carries with it no implications about abortion. The connection between the definition, whatever it is, and policy can come only from arguments that are outside science itself.

A good deal of the rest of this book is devoted to examining the relevant areas of science to determine exactly when humanness, in the sense that we use the term, enters the picture. The period corresponding to the onset of the functioning of the cerebral cortex (at about twenty-four to thirty-two weeks) is a compelling candidate for the acquisition of humanness.

Humanness and Abortion

Obviously, we would not have gone to the trouble of writing a book like this if our only purpose was to introduce a new term to the abortion debate. We believe that the concept of humanness has important implications in that debate. We have to stress, however, that reasoning from science to policy implications is a separate act from the scientific thought that goes into determining when the onset of humanness occurs.

The connection we see arises from a simple observation. There would be no abortion debate if abortion did not involve a conflict of rights. From the point of view of abortion rights advocates, what is at stake is the right of an adult person to control the decisions that affect her. This is a right that is highly prized in American culture. From the point of view of opponents of abortion, what is at stake is the right of an unborn fetus to live. If one believes, as they do, that the fetus is a person at conception, then this, too, is a highly prized right. The problem, of course, is that in a situation where the woman desires an abortion, both rights cannot be exercised at the same time.

The crucial point is what or who is exercising the respective rights. The woman, of course, is an adult human being, a person. The fetus, on the other hand, changes daily, rapidly acquiring new characteristics and properties all the time. Before it has acquired humanness, however, it does not possess those properties that distinguish humans from other animals. Therefore, the conflict of rights is between someone who has acquired the property of humanness and an entity that has not.

In such a situation, it seems obvious to us that the presumption must be on the side of the woman—that the rights of a person who has acquired humanness must prevail over those of a fetus or embryo that has not.

After the fetus has acquired humanness, however, the situation is changed. Here we have a conflict between two beings, both of whom have this property in some degree. In this situation, there is no longer a clear assumption of right on either side. In essence, the issue becomes undecidable from a science-based argument, and other means of resolving the conflict must be brought in.

This argument can be made no matter when humanness is acquired. If, for example, one can show that it is acquired at conception, then the argument above is trivial: the rights of woman and the unborn must always be balanced. It is only if it occurs at a later time that our argument has policy implications, since it fixes a time before which abortion is totally a choice of the woman and after which the state has an interest in that choice.

Conception and Birth

One of the reasons we want to introduce the notion of humanness is that it can free public discourse from its preoccupation with conception and birth. These two points, one marking the beginning of pregnancy and the other the end, are dramatic and easily recognizable. They make easy references for purposes of debate and argument.

Between them lies a nine-month period of continual change and development, a period in which it is hard to draw discrete boundaries. The easiest thing to do is to choose one of the discrete, easily identifiable events, declare it to be special, and use it to mark the advent of personhood.

When any other point in development is proposed as a dividing line, an unavoidable ambiguity—a gray area—is associated with it. It's a little like trying to define the income at which someone stops being poor. No matter what income is chosen, it can always be argued that someone making one dollar more is just as poor as someone making one dollar less. This doesn't mean that the concepts *rich* and *poor* are meaningless, just that their boundaries are not sharply defined.

In just the same way, the advent of humanness is not a process that has a sharp boundary. Nonetheless, we will argue that there is a period of several weeks during which the property of humanness is being acquired. This is a sufficiently sharp dividing line to serve as a basis for decisions about the abortion issue.

With these thoughts in mind, we now turn to an examination of the nature of humanness and the place of human beings in the natural world.

CHAPTER 2

The Web of Life

There has been life on earth almost as long as there has been a planet. Over the millennia, living things have grown ever more complex, ever more able to fill every niche capable of supporting life. Living organisms range in complexity from single-celled bacteria floating in pond water to elephants roaming the plains of Africa. Every one affects, and is affected by, all the others. Over the past century and a half humans have come to understand that we, too, are part of this complex web of life—that we are related, in the deepest sense of the word, to every other organism on earth. The impact of modern biology on the abortion debate depends on being able to understand exactly what human beings share with other living things and what things differentiate us from them. If we want to know what makes us unique among living organisms, we have to begin by knowing what makes us the same as other organisms.

One way of assigning some sort of order to the complexity

of life is to examine living organisms and group them together according to the way they are built and the way they function. This was the classical task of the science of biology. The basic scheme is simple (at least in principle). Organisms are classified according to how much they resemble each other: human beings are more like gorillas than rabbits, more like rabbits than sand crabs, more like sand crabs than carrots, and so on. One can think of the results of this kind of sorting, which we usually associate with the eighteenth-century Swedish scientist Carolus Linnaeus, as putting each type of living thing on its own branch of a huge tree, with successive branchings away from the main trunk corresponding to finer and finer distinctions.

The main trunk of the tree splits into five main branches, called *kingdoms*. These are, respectively, the monera (single-celled organisms without nuclei, such as bacteria and blue-green algae), protistacta (simple organisms whose cells have nuclei, like the amoebas and the slime molds), fungi, plants, and animals. The living things within each of these great branches are more like each other than they are like those in the others, and there are specific criteria for deciding which kingdom a given organism belongs to. Plants, for example, transform and store the sun's energy through the process of photosynthesis, while most animals are mobile and get their energy by eating plants or each other.

Even at this most fundamental branching, there is a crucial distinction between forms of life. Plants, fungi, and animals all reproduce by combining genetic material from two parent organisms. Monera reproduce by a simple process of cell division, usually with no mixing of genetic material. And protistacta can reproduce either by simple division or by somewhat more complex processes in which separate cells merge genetic material.

In many multicelled organisms (including humans), there is

an important division of labor among cells, a division crucial to the process of reproduction. Most of the cells in an organism play a role in carrying out specific functions—waste disposal or energy transformation, for example. These cells have a full complement of genetic material. Some cells, however, have only half the normal complement. These are cells that figure in reproduction. The general term for these latter cells is *gamete*, but we will refer to them more often by the familiar terms *egg* and *sperm*. They come together in the process of reproduction, one from the male, one from the female, and each contributes half of the offspring's genetic material.

Within the animal kingdom, there are further branchings of the tree of life. One of the main problems faced by mobile multicellular organisms is communications between their various parts. If a worm is to crawl in a certain direction (or a human is to run), there has to be a way for cells in one part of the animal to be aware of and respond quickly to things happening in cells elsewhere. Specialized cells have been developed to carry out this task. We discuss these nerve cells in more detail in Chapter 6, but we note here only that all but the simplest animals have them, and that these cells in different animals are remarkably similar.

In many animals, nerve functions are concentrated in the front region, or head, in a rudimentary brain. In a small percentage of these animals, nerve cells are also organized to form a long chord down the animal's back, and in most cases this chord is protected by a backbone. Human beings, of course, are a member of this last group of animals, which is called the subphylum of *vertebrates*. We can think of "vertebrateness" as constituting an important branching on the tree of life.

Subsequent branchings become more technical and specialized. We are, for example, placental mammals: warm-blooded, hairy animals that give live birth and whose females possess special organs that produce milk to suckle the young. The next branching puts us into the order of primates, which we share with monkeys and apes, and which is characterized by (among other things) the possession of grasping fingers and toes, relatively large brains, eyes located at the front of the head, and, consequently, stereoscopic vision. The final branchings into family (hominid), genus (*Homo*), and species (*sapiens*) are a little unusual in the tree of life, because all other members of our family and genus are extinct (we'll return to this point in Chapter 4 when we discuss evolution). Other animals don't have such a barren neighborhood around their branches in the tree of life. The housecat, jaguar, and lynx, for example, are different species within the genus *Felis*.

When we use this sort of branching analysis, every living thing can be assigned a place on the tree, and those properties that distinguish one species from another can be inferred. This classification scheme fails to address one important question, however. While it can tell us the ways in which organisms differ from each other, it cannot tell us why these differences exist, nor can it illuminate the essential relatedness of every branch of the tree. To delve into these sorts of questions, we have to look beyond the outward appearances of living things and get down to their most basic aspects. In other words, we will have to look at the cells and molecules of which all living things are made.

Before doing so, however, we should point out something that will become more important later on. The organization of living things into a tree with branches, as well as the chemical unity we are about to discuss, both follow from one fact: All life on earth evolved from one common ancestor (see Chapter 4). If we appear to be related to other living things, it is because we come from the same stock.

When we consider the molecular basis of life, we find that

in spite of the incredible complexity and diversity of living things on our planet, there are some simple general statements that apply to everything: (1) All living things are made of cells; (2) the working of all cells is based on the chemical reactions of a similar group of molecules; and (3) all life is governed by the same genetic code.

These seemingly innocuous statements contain within them one of the central truths of modern science: All forms of life are related to each other, and the basic mechanisms that drive all of them are the same.

A note to the reader is in order at this point. The rest of this chapter is devoted to a more detailed discussion and justification of the statements just made. Those not wishing to go through these arguments can skip to Chapter 3, although we would suggest that every reader look at Table 1 on page 38, where numerical estimates of molecular overlap between humans and other living things are given.

Perhaps the best way to grasp the basic chemical unity underlying all life is to note that 95 percent of the mass of all cells is composed of molecules made of the same fifty basic building blocks. Just as the tallest skyscraper and the lowliest garage can be made by putting together different combinations of the same building materials, so can the most complex living things be built from the basic molecules of life. There is diversity of cells, but a unity of the things from which cells are made.

For example, there is a class of molecules called *carbohydrates* that figure prominently in the transformation and storage of energy in cells; some familiar examples are the sugar in beets, the complex carbohydrates in corn, and the glycogen that stores energy in human livers. These molecules also form into long cross-linked fibers, such as cellulose, that give plants their rigidity. All carbohydrates are made from a few building blocks called *sugars*, simple molecules built around rings of six carbon atoms. Hook together two different kinds of these molecules (called *fructose* and *glucose*), and you get ordinary table sugar. Make a long string of glucose molecules hooking certain parts of their rings together, and you get cellulose, the material that stiffens plant fibers and is used, among other things, to make materials like the paper on the page you are reading. Make a string of glucose molecules by hooking together different parts of the sugar rings, and you get the carbohydrates in that spaghetti you ate the other day, the ones your cells may be using for energy right now. From simple sugars can be made an enormous variety of different molecules important in the operation of living systems.

Not only are all living cells built from the same basic building blocks, but many of their basic functions operate in the same way. For example, every living thing needs to transform energy to sustain itself. If you look inside individual cells in any living thing, you will find a complex set of interactions whose function is to package this energy by processing basic materials. For example, in plants, photosynthesis takes energy from the sun and produces glucose, one of the sugars we just discussed. In animals like humans, this sugar is released by the breaking down of complex molecules in food. It is the chemical processing (think "burning") of glucose that supplies the energy the cell needs to operate. Some cells may acquire their glucose by ingestion, others by photosynthesis but in all of them the basic mechanism by which they make use of energy is the same.

Think of it this way: In our economy, all sorts of different transactions go on. People buy cars, sell food, trade their services. But in all of these various transactions, there is one thing—money—that appears over and over again. No matter what the transaction, money serves as the universal medium of exchange. In the same way, energy in cells comes from all sorts of sources and is used to perform all sorts of functions, but at the very heart of the energy transaction, we find the same set of molecules acting as the medium of barter. These molecules, which go by technical names like *adenosine triphosphate* and *nicotinamide adenine dinucleotide*, show up in the energy transactions in all cells. They are the universal energy coinage of life, something humans share with all other living things. The fact that both you and the amoeba use these universal molecules in your energy metabolism is as striking an example of the relatedness of life as can be found.

Proteins and the Genetic Code

Cells have to do something with the energy they extract from the environment. In your body each cell has a specialized function it must perform to make the body function as a whole. The cells in your pancreas, for example, produce insulin that your body uses to control the digestion of sugar, and the liver produces bile to help digest fats. Other chemical reactions produce materials needed in the operation and upkeep of the cells. In every cell, some chemical reactions take place that tear down molecules derived from food to provide the cell's energy, and other reactions take place that use this energy to keep the cell and the organism of which it is part operating. Modern biochemists, in fact, think that the best analogy to a living cell is not a shapeless blob of protoplasm, but something like a complex factory or chemical-processing plant. At the bottom, it is the chemical reactions in the cell that keep every living thing going, and it is this fact that explains our statement that all life is based on related chemical reactions.

But the important activities in the cell don't involve random chemical processes. Because there are so many reactions that could take place, the cell needs help to pick out those that are needed—help provided by special molecules called *enzymes*.

The problem is this: Although molecules in the cells are built up from simple modules, they can get quite large and complex in shape. When two such molecules come together, only a few parts of one can actually attach to corresponding parts on the other. Think of these as sticky spots on each molecule. An enzyme is a third molecule that, while not actually changing the reaction itself, attaches itself to each of the first two molecules in such a way that their sticky parts come together. After they do, the enzyme lets go and moves off, unaffected, to play the same role elsewhere. Without the presence of the enzyme, no reaction occurs.

In living systems, the enzymes that drive the cell's reactions are proteins. These molecules are the real workhorses of life. They provide a good deal of the material that supplies the structural strength of cells—your hair and fingernails are made from them, for example. But more important, they are crucial in the operation of the cell's chemistry.

Like other important molecules, proteins are complex molecules that are made up by the stringing together of simple modules. In the case of proteins, these modules are some twenty different molecules called *amino acids*. An amino acid is made of ten to twenty or so atoms of carbon, nitrogen, oxygen, sulfur, and hydrogen. For our purposes, think of each of them as a core with a nitrogen–hydrogen combination projecting from one side and an oxygen–hydrogen combination projecting from the other (the various amino acids differ in the nature of the molecular structures that are attached to the core). When two amino acids come together, the hydrogen from the nitrogen–hydrogen side of one bonds to the hydrogen–oxygen combination of the other to form a molecule of water (H_2O), leaving the bodies of the two amino acids locked together. This process can be repeated at both ends of the new molecule, so that the amino acids can be strung together virtually without end. The resulting chain of amino acids is a protein.

What makes these chains so important in cellular chemistry is that after they are formed, they fold up into a complex three-dimensional shape. Think of each protein as a kind of molecular beanbag, with all sorts of hills and valleys in its surface. It is these hills and valleys that allow proteins to play the role of enzymes. A given protein is shaped so that each of the two interacting molecules fits snugly into some crinkle in its surface. In this way, the protein locks onto the two molecules and holds them together while they form their bonds. When they do so, the resulting molecule no longer has the same shape as its two predecessors, so it no longer fits into the original patterns on the protein surface. It will therefore float off, leaving the protein free to start the process all over again. These sorts of simple, protein-driven enzymatic reactions are part of what makes life possible.

Understanding this, we now come to the concept that is the basis of the modern comprehension of life. Every reaction in the cell requires a different protein to act as an enzyme: no protein, no reaction. The protein's suitability for a given reaction depends on its shape, and this shape, in turn, depends on the precise sequence of amino acids that were strung together to make the protein in the first place. Change even one amino acid in that sequence, and you change the hills and valleys on the resulting protein and, in all likelihood, destroy its usefulness as an enzyme for the original reaction.

So the question of how a cell works comes down to something very simple: How does the cell know the proper sequence for the amino acids that it puts together when it is making proteins? It is to answer this question that we turn to what is probably the most famous biological molecule: deoxyribonucleic acid, or DNA. It is this molecule that contains the blueprint for making all of the proteins that drive reactions in cells, and which therefore amply justifies its nickname "the molecule of life."

The actual structure of DNA is a double helix (see Figure 1), but it's easier to understand how it works by imagining it to be a ladder. (You can twist it back into the double helix shape in your mind once we've gone through the basics.) The sides of the ladder are made of alternating molecules of a sugar (deoxyribose, from which the molecule gets part of its name) and a molecule (phosphate) made of a combination of hydrogen, phosphorous, and oxygen. The important parts of the molecule, from our point of view, are the rungs of the ladder. They are made by joining together molecules (called *bases*) that stick out of the sides of the sugar molecules and lock together. Four different bases occur in DNA: guanine (G), cytosine (C), thymine (T), and adenine (A).

The important thing about the bases isn't so much their names or the details of how they are built, but the fact that they are shaped so that each of them can bind only to one other. For example, T can bind to A, but not to itself, G, or C. Similarly, G can bind to C, but not to itself, T, or A. Thus, the rungs of the DNA ladder are made up of only four kinds of base combination: A-T, T-A, C-G, and G-C. If you read down one side of the ladder, you will find a sequence of bases that make up that side of the rungs—TTGTGACACAT, for example. It is this sequence that we call the *genetic message*. Ultimately, the genetic message is what tells the cell which proteins to make.

In some cases, the DNA is coiled up in the body of the cell. Such cells are called *prokaryotes* ("before the nucleus"). In the human body (and all other advanced life forms), however, the DNA is contained in a special structure called the *nucleus*,

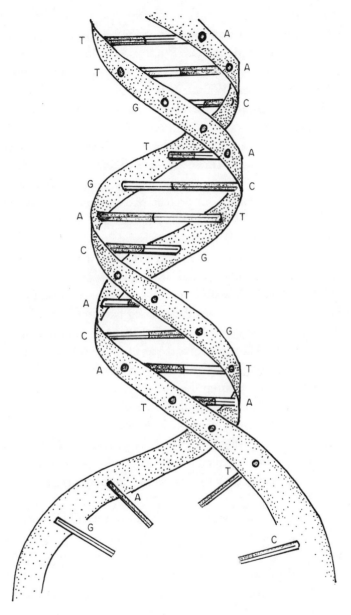

Figure 1

which is separated from the rest of the cell by a membrane. Such cells are called *eukaryotes* ("true nuclei"). In human beings, the DNA in the nucleus is contained in forty-six separate strings called *chromosomes*. Within each chromosome the DNA is coiled and wrapped on a series of cores, more or less like tape in a tape recorder.

In the DNA on each chromosome are sequences of bases known as *genes*. Each of these sequences contains the information needed to assemble the sequence of amino acids for one protein – one gene, one protein; one protein, one reaction. The way the cell "reads" the genetic code is this: A special enzyme moves along the outside of the DNA double helix, and when it gets to the segment that constitutes the gene, it starts to separate the base pairs from one another. Think of it as "unzipping" the segment of DNA. Directed by a number of other enzymes, a series of small molecules then hook onto the exposed bases to form a larger molecule called *messenger RNA* (mRNA), the initials standing for *ribonucleic acid*. The sequence of the small molecules preserves the information in the sequence of bases on the original DNA. The mRNA then moves from the nucleus to the body of the cell, where, with the help of still other molecules, it assembles a chain of amino acids whose sequence is dictated by the sequence of bases on the original gene in the DNA. When the amino acids have been strung together, the protein folds up, forms its hills and valleys, and goes on to act as an enzyme or to perform some other function.

It turns out that three contiguous bases on the mRNA (called a *codon*) determine the identity of one amino acid in the final protein. A codon composed of GCA, for example, will be "read" as the amino acid called *alanine* in the final protein. Each of the sixty-four possible combinations of three bases can be interpreted in a similar way.

In this way, the sequence of bases on the DNA, which are

read out into sequences on mRNA, can be though of as a language, or a coded message, written in triplets. In what is one of the most astonishing discoveries in the history of science, biologists in this century have found that virtually all living things use precisely the same genetic code to assemble their proteins.

The fact that all living things use the same code, of course, doesn't mean that they all write the same messages. After all, all of us use the "code" of English spelling, but everything we write isn't the same. This distinction allows us to make a sweeping statement about the relatedness between different living things: *The hereditary differences between different living things is contained in the differences between the sequences of bases in their DNA.*

Having said this, we have to make one important point. Not all the DNA in any organism actually codes for proteins. In humans, for example, only about 5 percent of the DNA is actually contained in the genes. The function of the rest isn't fully known at this time, but scientists believe that it contains, among other things, instructions about when genes are to be used to make proteins (or, in the language of biologists, when they are to be "expressed"). For example, every cell in your body contains the message for making insulin, but only cells in your pancreas actually "express" the gene. The question of how genes are turned on and off (or "controlled") is an important field of current research, one we'll return to in the next chapter.

The Similarities and the Differences

There are about three billion base pairs in all the human DNA contained on our chromosomes, or about a billion triplets. Among these base pairs, there are genes for a few tens of thousands of proteins, although only a few thousand at most are made at a given time in a given cell. The sum total of all of this coding is called the *human genome*. You can imagine comparing strands of DNA from closely related species by laying them out and reading them. (The actual techniques used are somewhat more complex.)

If you were to compare one human being to another, the differences in the DNA sequences would be too small to be resolved by the normal techniques, although researchers have been able to see differences in specific genes. A difference of one base pair in many hundred in the gene for hemoglobin, for example, is the only difference between a person with the sickle-cell anemia trait and a person without it.

Yet these sorts of tiny differences in DNA are what produces all the diversity we find among human beings. They make one person tall, another short; they give one person blue eyes, another brown, and so on. It doesn't take much of a difference in the genome, in other words, to produce enormous differences in the individuals possessing those genomes.

One way of gauging the relatedness between living things—of saying how much one organism resembles another—is to ask how much their respective DNA sequences overlap. If, for example, we carried out the operation with DNA outlined above for a human being and a chimpanzee (our closest living relation), we would find that coding portions of the two strands of DNA differ by only 3 base pairs in 200; that is, there is a 98.5 percent identity. This difference is considerably larger than the differences between individual humans, but the DNA differences between us and the chimpanzees are still pretty small. As we get farther and farther away from the human branch on the tree of life, the overlaps between strands of DNA get smaller and smaller.

Except for a few species of organisms commonly used in

laboratories, there is little information about the sequence of bases in DNA in other species. The full human genome itself is not known. There is ongoing effort to do the work necessary to obtain this knowledge called the Human Genome Project, and it is a subject of much scientific, not to mention political, debate. Consequently, if we want to know about the relationship of human beings to other forms of life, we have to compromise a bit. Instead of looking at DNA directly, we can compare the sequences of amino acids in related proteins in different organisms. Since this sequence is determined by the genetic code, it ought to provide a good measure of the overlap in DNA. In principle, it should make no more difference whether we compare amino acid sequences in proteins or DNA sequences directly, any more than it makes a difference whether we look at a photograph or a negative. (A word of warning: Because there are sixty-four possible triplets of base pairs and only twenty amino acids, there is a certain amount of redundancy in the genetic code; that is, more than one triplet can code for a given amino acid. Scientists call this the "degeneracy" of the code. This means that we can't necessarily unambiguously go from an amino acid in a protein back to the genetic message.)

It turns out that a fair amount of work has been done in finding the sequences of amino acids in important proteins in many species. A good deal of this research is aimed at elucidating the relationships between different organisms and deciding how they evolved. Regardless of the motivation, however, we can use the data to make our point about the essential relatedness of living things.

Part of the energy metabolism of every living cell is a protein called *cytochrome-C*. This is a modestly sized protein, containing only 104 amino acids. It is involved in transferring energy from the "burning" process to the "energy coinage" we discussed earlier. It is performing this function right now in most of the cells in your body.

If you line up a molecule of cytochrome-C from a human being with the corresponding molecule from a chimpanzee, you can compare down the chains, one amino acid at a time, and see how they match. If you did this matching, you would find the overlap to be 100 percent; that is, the molecule in the chimpanzee is exactly the same as it is in humans.

You can make a similar comparison with any other organism. Table 1 shows the results for a selection of living things.

The key point here is that this particular stretch of amino acids, concerned with a basic function of the living cell, is very similar for a remarkable variety of living things. You have to go from human beings to insects, for example, before the overlap drops below 75 percent. Even for yeast, a single-celled organism, it is above 50 percent.

Different organisms may look very different; there is certainly no obvious connection between a human being and a

Table 1. *Comparison of Cytochrome-C between Humans and Other Organisms*

Organism	Overlap with human cytochrome-C (%)
Chimpanzee	100
Dog	90
Rattlesnake	86
Tuna	77
Fruit fly	73
Pumpkin	71
Brewer's yeast	58

pumpkin. Yet if you ignore the outward appearances and come down to the basic working unit of life, the cell, you find an unexpected unity. At the chemical level, human beings just aren't all that different from pumpkins or any other life forms. The most fundamental chemical reactions in cells proceed pretty much the same way in all living things. We share these basic functions with all of life.

3

The Biology of
Conception

Much of the controversy in the abortion debate centers on the statement "Life begins at conception." In the minds of many people there is something unique, something singular about conception—something that makes it a special event in the chain of events leading to birth. There's no point in trying to dodge this issue or pretend it doesn't exist. In fact, our experience in discussing abortion with others has been that unless we deal with conception first, it is difficult to go on to the rest of the points we wish to make in this book.

There are really two issues that must be grappled with in any discussion of the nature of conception: First, we need to know exactly what it is and how it fits into the sequence of events that produce a new human life. Thus we need an understanding of some basic (and well-known) biology. Second, we have to ask whether we can single out conception as a radically discontinuous event. We will argue that conception is just one link in a chain of events.

We recognize that to many people such a statement of cold biological fact misses something essential about the developing fetus. We recognize that there is a strong inclination to assign personhood or a soul to the single cell that results from fertilization on the grounds that it represents "potential life." Our position is that this inclination, as strongly as it may be favored on religious or social grounds, has no basis in science because, as we point out in Chapter 1, personhood and soul are simply not scientific concepts. The strongest argument we can make rests on recent and ongoing research in the area of parthenogenesis—the process by which unfertilized (rather than fertilized) eggs can be made to give rise to new members of a species. This work will soon confront those who hold to the "potential life" argument with an insurmountable difficulty. They will either have to accord every unfertilized egg—eggs now routinely lost prior to menstruation—the same status as potential life that they accord the product of conception, or they will have to move the point they consider special to some other place in the sequence.

The end point of this reasoning is that any policy based on assigning a unique status to conception in the emergence of humanness must be seen as coming from subjective evaluations—evaluations that may not be shared by others. Subjectivity does not, of course, make these arguments wrong; it simply means that they cannot be given the kind of public universality we assign to arguments grounded in scientific understanding.

The Biology of Conception

The genetic inheritance that you contribute to your children began to assemble when you were a three-week-old embryo in your mother's uterus. At that time a group of cells broke off from the wall of the yolk sac and migrated into the forming embryo, taking up positions that were, later on, appropriate to germ cells—cells that produce the eggs and sperm through which humans reproduce.

In females, these germ cells go to work almost immediately, producing a supply of eggs that will last a woman throughout her entire life. Each mature egg contains half the genetic material (DNA) found in a normal human body cell as well as some small DNA containing structures, called *mitochondria*, that play a role in the processing of energy in cells.* Most of the immature eggs die as the fetus develops, is born, and enters early childhood. At birth, a typical human female has about a million eggs stored in her ovaries; at puberty, 400,000 have survived. Of these, only about 500 will eventually be released by ovulation, one at a time, and therefore have a chance of taking part in reproduction during the woman's lifetime.

After puberty, a single egg matures each four weeks. This egg is surrounded by other cells in a structure formed by a thickening in the wall of the ovary. Once during each menstrual cycle, one of these structures splits open and an egg is released in the process of ovulation. It is this release that signals the possibility of a pregnancy.

While all of this development is going on in the female, from fetus to adulthood, the germ cell generators in the male during the maturing period have been relatively quiescent. After puberty, they continuously produce the cells that eventually develop into mobile sperm. Like the egg nucleus, each sperm nucleus contains half the genetic material found in a normal human body cell.

The act of fertilization actually takes place in the Fallopian tube, which connects the ovary to the uterus. Many sperm attach themselves to a typical egg and, through chemical action,

*There is a short review of the role of DNA in living systems in the section titled "Proteins and the Genetic Code" in Chapter 2.

start to break down the egg's protective outer membrane. Eventually, one sperm gets through. It then breaks down, leaving a single nucleus with its allotment of DNA. The nuclei of the egg and the sperm merge, producing a new nucleus containing a full complement of genetic material. This material, in the form of DNA molecules and other structures in the egg, contains all the internal instructions necessary for the single cell to develop into an adult human being.

The single cell resulting from the fertilization of the egg is called a *zygote*. During the next four days, two things happen: First, the zygote continues its journey down the Fallopian tube into the uterus, and, second, it starts to divide. By the time the cell and its descendants reach the uterus, the original zygote has grown to some eight or sixteen cells. During the next two days, a few more divisions occur, and the system acquires both a specialized structure and a special name. It's called a *blastocyst*, and you can think of it as being something like a thick-walled hollow sphere with a swelling at one point. In cross section, it looks something like a class ring with a heavy stone (see Figure 2). The stone contains the cells that will eventually develop into the embryo, and the sphere contains cells that will eventually develop, along with material from the mother, into the placenta. Six days after fertilization, the blastocyst implants itself in the wall of the uterus.

In general, the term *embryo* is used to describe the system after implantation; *fetus*, to describe it after sixty days.

Is Conception Special?

Even with this abbreviated sketch of the process of fertilization, one thing is obvious. When biologists object to statements about life beginning at conception, they are not splitting hairs or being pedantic. There is no time in the sequence we've just

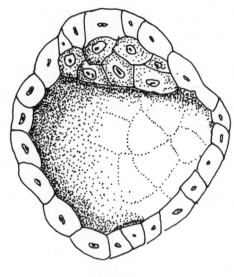

BLASTOCYST

Figure 2

described where new life is created. In fact, from the point of view of the biologist, *at conception, two previously existing living things come together to form another living thing.*

Look at it this way: The DNA in the egg and the sperm that come together at conception were not formed from nothing but can be traced back to a time before the birth of the parents. In fact, as we see in Chapter 4, biologists tend to look at life as a single seamless web going back almost four billion years, to the first cell formed on our planet. Nevertheless, two things about the event of conception are often cited as providing evidence that it marks the beginning of the life of the individual:

1. At conception, two collections of DNA, each of which existed previously, come together in a new combination, one that has not previously existed. To be more precise, this combi-

nation comes into existence at the moment when the nucleus of the sperm merges with that of the egg. The start of the individual human life is then taken to be the moment when this new collection of molecules forms.

2. At conception, for the first time, we have a situation in which an adult human life *could* develop. If you just leave the system alone, the argument goes, it will eventually result in a live birth. In our experience, this is the most common justification for designating conception as the start of human life. Call it the *argument from possibility*.

To these sorts of widely held views, we can make two sorts of rejoinders. First, we can point out that they do not really mesh well with the way that biologists think about their science these days. This sort of argument tends to be general, rather than specific. Second, we can point to ongoing research that undermines the notion of the zygote as the only entity for which the "possible life" argument can be made. If we can find other systems that are "potential life" in the same sense as the zygote, but that are not usually accorded special status, we will necessarily weaken the notion that there is something singular about the moment of conception itself.

General Arguments

The Genetic Information Is a Blueprint, Not a Building

After fertilization the zygote contains a complete set of human chromosomes, each made of a stretch of DNA. On these chromosomes is the information used to make each of the thousands of proteins needed to grow and maintain the human body, as well as the information that tells the developing cell when each of those genes is to be activated.

Does this information make the zygote a "potential life"? It does, but only in the sense that a blueprint is a potential building. Just as a whole constellation of workers and materials are needed to turn blueprints into a skyscraper, a great deal of machinery and material is needed to turn the zygote into a full-term baby. This machinery tends to be invisible to us, of course, because it is located inside the mother's body, but it is there nonetheless. There is a great deal of truth in the T shirt worn by pregnant women, the one with an arrow pointing toward the abdomen and a sign saying "Construction Zone."

We do not ordinarily assign the date of the completion of the blueprints a special place of honor in the construction of a building. In the same way, we argue, we should not assign the assembling of the DNA a special place in the development of a human being.

The Zygote Is Not All That Unique

The idea that the new combination of DNA is unique is, in our view, a rather weak way to support the idea that life begins at conception. Although it is true that conception marks the first appearance of this exact combination of DNA in the species lineage, we do not normally give this uniqueness much reverence in the rest of our lives. Every day, for example, large amounts of human tissue are excised in the operating rooms of the nation's hospitals. Every single cell in this tissue carries precisely the same genetic blueprint as the zygote from which the patient developed, yet we do not accord it any legal or moral protection. In fact, after it has been examined by a pathologist, it is usually tossed into a container marked "Medical Waste," hauled off, and incinerated.

Nor does genetic uniqueness, in and of itself, normally command our respect. Tumors that grow in the human body carry as unique a genetic blueprint as does a new zygote, yet we destroy those tumors as best we can. In fact, we could say that the purpose of medical treatment in this case is to make sure that the genetic blueprint of the tumor doesn't survive. We value the uniqueness of individuals with humanness, but that is not the same as valuing the uniqueness of genetic information.

To be consistent with biological understanding at the molecular level, the "unique blueprint" argument would require that we allow tumors to grow. To our knowledge, no one has advocated this point of view, and we can see no biologically reasonable way of applying the argument only to a zygote.

The Probability of Success of the Zygote Is Low

If the egg–sperm system is believed to become a potential life at the moment of conception, then it is reasonable to ask how potential that life is. If, for example, it should turn out that only one zygote in a thousand results in a full-term pregnancy, the argument that every zygote deserves full legal protection would be considerably weakened. If, on the other hand, there were a virtual certainty that every conception would lead to a viable pregnancy, this aspect of the argument from possibility would be strengthened.

Data on the outcomes of conception are hard to come by. No one knows, for example, how many late periods result from early miscarriages and how many from temporary dysfunctions in the menstrual cycle. Nevertheless, there are some estimates of these numbers, and if anything, these estimates probably overstate the chance of success. The best way to understand these data is to think of the sequence of events outlined above and ask what the chances are that each stage will be gotten through successfully.

There is no information on how many successful mergers there are between sperm and egg nuclei, nor on how likely it is that the resulting zygote will actually start the process of cell division and then complete the trip down the Fallopian tube and wind up as a blastocyst. We will be conservative and assume that there is a 100 percent success rate at this stage of development, but keep in mind that this almost certainly is a large overestimate of the actual rate. The next step involves the implantation of the blastocyst in the wall of the uterus. Many things can go wrong here: the cell division in the zygote may not proceed properly, the blastocyst may not implant properly, or it may implant in the wrong place (in the Fallopian tube, for example, the result being a tubal pregnancy). The net result is that only about 75 percent of the zygotes actually implant themselves in the uterine walls. Of these, only about 60 percent survive to the end of the second week of gestation. In other words, even if we assume that the blastocyst stage is always attained, only about 45 percent (60 percent of 75 percent) of the fertilized eggs lead to results in which a woman will miss her first menstrual period and realize she is pregnant.

Finally (and here the data are somewhat better), only about 72 percent of pregnancies that have gone as far as a missed period result in live births.

The net result is that slightly fewer than a third of all conceptions (72 percent of 45 percent) lead to a fetus that has a chance of developing. In other words, if you were to choose a zygote at random and follow it through the first week of development, the chances are less than one in three that it would still be there at full term, *even though there has been no human intervention.* Nature, it seems, performs abortions at a much higher rate than any human society. It is simply not true that most zygotes, if undisturbed, will produce a human being. The probability that a conception will result in a live birth is actually quite low. Note that since we have assumed that all conceptions lead to cell division, we have almost surely overestimated the true success rate.

The Potential of the Unfertilized Egg

To our minds, the strongest evidence against the "life begins at conception" viewpoint comes from experiments reported in the scientific literature on parthenogenesis, the creation of a viable fetus from an unfertilized egg. The implications of this work strike at the heart of the potential-life argument, because they tell us that an unfertilized egg can, under the right circumstances, be as full of life potential as a zygote. Since we do not normally consider an unfertilized egg worthy of special treatment — no one, for example, mourns a woman's period just because it involves the loss of such an egg — it follows that we should not do so for a zygote either.

We should say up front that experiments of the type we will describe have never been done on humans (and probably would never be allowed). Nevertheless, they can be done on laboratory animals whose physiology is sufficiently like ours to make the extrapolation to humans reasonable. We should also point out that in some species, such as the whip-tailed lizard, parthenogenesis is not at all unusual and is, in fact, the normal mode of reproduction.

In one of the classical experiments of biology, exposing frog eggs to salt water was shown to start the process of growth that leads to tadpoles and frogs, even if no sperm is present. In this case, the unfertilized eggs are clearly potential life. This sort of straightforward production of adults from unfertilized eggs can be done routinely in reptiles, amphibians, and birds. There are two reports in the scientific literature of similar experiments on mammals. One, involving rabbits, proceeded by stimulating an unfertilized egg until it started to divide, then implanting it in the uterus. The other involved a more complex set of procedures on a special strain of mice. Since neither of these experiments has been duplicated in spite of numerous attempts, however, we do not want to cite them as examples of successful parthenogenesis.

The real question, of course, is whether this sort of procedure (or some more complicated analogue) can be made to work routinely on mammals like ourselves. Over the past few years, the study of how fertilization and embryonic development work in mammals has become a hot topic, and some rather amazing insights have been achieved. These results bear on the question of the role of conception in producing life.

In current experiments on mice, the basic technique is to wait until the nucleus of the unfertilized egg divides (which it does only in special strains of laboratory animals) and then to allow the two nuclei to recombine as if one had come from a sperm. The same effect could be achieved by stimulating an unfertilized egg so that it divides, then removing the nucleus from one of the resulting cells and inserting it into the other. Once a full complement of DNA is present, the system is allowed to develop into a blastocyst, which is then implanted in the uterine wall and allowed to grow. The same sort of manipulation can be done in the laboratory to produce an egg with DNA from a sperm only, or to produce DNA that has been altered in various ways. The usual scenario is that the implanted cells start to divide and grow but spontaneously abort at a stage that would correspond to a sixty-day fetus in a human being.

The problem appears to be that in the absence of sperm, the parthenogenic eggs seem to be unable to induce the proper development of the placenta. It appears that most of the instructions for the development of that particular structure are carried by the sperm, and that these instructions are not available in the parthenogenic egg. Thus the egg can start dividing but cannot provide itself with a full placenta (and hence cannot provide the developing embryo with the nourishment it needs to survive). The reason that parthenogenesis in amphibians, reptiles, and birds proceeds without encountering this problem, of course, is that the placenta is not part of the developmental process in those organisms.

DNA from males and females contains genes for the same functions (although the genes themselves need not be identical). The most likely way that male–female asymmetry arises is for something to happen to DNA in the mother and the father so that when the sperm and the egg combine, they contribute differently to subsequent development. The current theory about how this happens is that some genes in the egg and the sperm were switched off while they were being formed, but switched off in different patterns in the two cells. For example, genes crucial to the development of the placenta may be left unmodified in the sperm's DNA but may be turned off in the egg. DNA that has been affected in this way is said to be *imprinted*.

Today, researchers are concentrating on the details of how imprinting works. The best explanation at the moment is that a group of atoms called a *methyl group*, consisting of a carbon and three attached hydrogens, hooks onto one of the C (cytosine) bases in the DNA molecule—not in a place that affects the bonding of the bases across the DNA "ladder," but on the side of the base and facing the sugar–phosphate spine. The methyl group causes the double helix to bulge out where it attaches (think of it as something like lint stuck in a zipper). The bulge prevents the production of the proteins coded for in the following stretch of DNA; in effect, it switches the gene (or a group of genes) off.

In the sperm, a certain sequence of genes has been turned off during maturation, while other sequences have been left on. The same thing happens in the egg, except that there is a different on-off sequence. Apparently some genes crucial for the development of the placenta have been turned off in the egg but left on in the sperm; this is why the simple attempts at parthenogenesis described above haven't been universally successful.

But consider this: We routinely manipulate DNA in our laboratories. Before long, researchers will have worked out the nature of the off-on sequence that governs the development of the placenta. Removing and inserting methyl groups into the DNA (moving lint in and out of the zipper) is a relatively straightforward operation. It is only a matter of time, then, before someone stimulates an unfertilized egg, lets it divide, removes the DNA from one cell, and resets the off-on sequence that allows development to go forward. When this happens— and we have little doubt that it will happen—we will have true parthenogenesis. We will be able to produce an adult human being from a single unfertilized egg.

There is nothing in this scenario that requires major new breakthroughs. Indeed, given the rate of advance in biotechnology, almost any time estimate for completion will probably turn out to be on the conservative side. So let's examine what happens to the possible-life argument when, in principle, a full-term fetus can be produced from a single unfertilized egg.

Imagine that you have a fertilized egg, a conventional zygote, in one test tube and an unfertilized egg in the other. Neither can develop into a human being by itself. Left to themselves, they would both perish. Each, however, has the potential of becoming a human being, *provided that it is supplied with the appropriate machinery.* In the case of the zygote, that machinery is the mother's body. In the case of the unfertilized egg, that machinery involves a laboratory and then the mother's body.

Those who argue that life begins at conception hold that the zygote is legally entitled to the use of the machinery it requires to realize its potential. By what criterion, then, would they deny that right to the unfertilized egg? Surely it is a much easier choice to grant the right to a laboratory procedure than to the use of someone's body. To be consistent, you would have to say either that both the zygote and the unfertilized egg are potential life and therefore are entitled to the use of life-giving machinery, or that neither is. There is no middle ground.

But isn't the machinery needed by the unfertilized egg unnatural? It is no more unnatural than the incubator used to keep a premature infant alive, and certainly less unnatural than *in utero* surgery. We are used to intervening during the course of a pregnancy to allow the embryo or fetus to achieve its full potential. By what right, then, do we refuse to intervene to allow an unfertilized egg to do so?

The only way to make a distinction is to say that a zygote is already in the uterus and thus has already appropriated the machinery. But this sort of argument simply begs the question around which the abortion debate centers, namely, the question of whether the woman or the fetus has the right to decide on the use of that machinery.

To find a scientific reason to support the possible-life argument, then, we have to agree that when the technology for parthenogenesis becomes available, it should be considered immoral to allow any unfertilized egg to go to waste. Every time a woman menstruates, a potential life has been cut off just as surely as when a zygote is killed. We do not normally worry about the moral consequences of the menstrual cycle, but if we accept the potential-life argument, we would have to.

In other words, since both the fertilized and the unfertilized eggs have the potential for life, the choice to extend legal protection to one and not the other must be based on some other criterion. It cannot be based on this potential alone.

The same sort of reasoning that we apply to the unfertilized egg can be applied to the cells that result from the first several divisions after fertilization. Implicit in the argument that the zygote represents a potential life is a view of embryonic development as a kind of lock-step progression from a single cell to a fully developed child—the idea that once fertilization has occurred, the human outcome is inevitable. In fact, there is a plasticity about the cells in the early development of the embryo that makes the outcome of fertilization far from certain.

For example, it is possible to take a cell from the blastocyst, remove its nucleus, and implant it in an unfertilized egg from which the original nucleus has been removed. This manipulated egg, if allowed to develop into a blastocyst and then planted in the wall of the uterus, will develop into a mature individual as easily as a normal zygote. This process, called *cloning,* is carried out routinely in laboratory animals, and most scientists believe it could, in principle, be carried out in humans as well.

Further evidence of plasticity in early development can be seen in multiple births. These result from a splitting of the original zygote into two or more separate cells, each of which initiates the development of a separate fetus.

If the zygote deserves protection because it is a potential life, there is a serious problem in denying that protection to every cell in the blastocyst. We have the technical capability to turn every fertilized egg into a virtually limitless number of human beings. If reverence for potential life is to serve as our moral guidepost, it is hard to see how we can justify not doing so.

Conception as Continuum

From a biological point of view, conception is one of a series of important events that have to take place before a child can be born. Without conception, there would be no child, of course, but the same can be said of almost any event in the scenario outlined above, from the formation of germ cells when the parents were themselves *in utero* to the implantation of the blastocyst in the uterine walls a week after fertilization.

In fact, given the high probability that the blastocyst will fail to implant and continue the pregnancy, you might want to designate implantation, rather than conception, as the beginning of "life." But the minute you admit this sort of possibility, you are, in fact, admitting that there is no particular scientific basis for singling out conception.

This doesn't mean you can't assign an arbitrary significance to conception. It is perfectly self-consistent to say something like "My religious convictions (or my political beliefs or my personal standards of morality) lead me to say that the fetus becomes a person (or acquires a soul) at the moment of conception and is therefore entitled to full protection from that time on." This argument is, in fact, made quite often in the abortion debate. All we are saying is that if you wish to argue in this way, you should realize that your opinion is based on a subjective standard, not on a scientific framework. You should, therefore, acknowledge that other people are not compelled to share your convictions and may freely choose other standards.

4

The Emergence of Humanness

We humans are part of the web of life, but we are different. We share a large part of our biochemistry with the housefly, but the housefly does not build pyramids or skyscrapers. There may be a large overlap between our energy-processing molecules and those of brewer's yeast, but brewer's yeast doesn't build spaceships or write novels. There was a time when biologists, obsessed with their newfound discovery of the links between humans and the rest of life, found themselves saying that there was virtually no difference between *Homo sapiens* and other living things. But this assertion is ridiculous on its face. You don't have to be a great scholar to see that humans are different; all you have to do is look around you.

The crux of our argument in this book is that it is possible to determine what it is that distinguishes us from other living things. We call these qualities *humanness*, and most of our attention later on will be focused on deciding when a developing fetus has acquired them. First, however, we have to determine exactly what those qualities are.

The most biologically reasonable way to make this sort of distinction is to look back at the history of life on our planet and see when our ancestors acquired the traits that go into making a human being. Some of these traits are shared with other species, but some are uniquely human. We will see that it was only a few million years ago — a mere blink of the eye in evolutionary time — that creatures appeared on this planet who could reason and make tools. Anatomically, they resembled their nearest relatives in most respects, but they walked erect and possessed enlarged outer layers in their brains, a structure called the *cerebral cortex*. Since the first ancestors with this attribute appeared, the history of human evolution has been marked by a more-or-less steady increase in the size of the cortex, accompanied by the development of ever more complex and sophisticated ways of dealing with the environment and each other. The acquisition of the enlarged cerebral cortex sets humankind off from the rest of the living world; it is the crucial difference we have been searching for.

Evolutionary Progress

When the earth first formed 4.5 billion years ago, it was hot and lifeless — sterile in the truest sense of the term. But within a relatively short time, geologically speaking, the borders of the oceans were teeming with living things. By a process imperfectly understood, the raw materials of the planet's surface had been collected into organized systems that could take energy from sunlight and use it to drive chemical reactions. These distant ancestors of ours were simple things: single-celled organisms with their DNA coiled up but not enclosed in a nucleus.

You can think of them as being similar to some of the photosynthetic bacteria that float in calm ponds today. They are the ancestors of the prokaryotes we discuss in Chapter 2.

Yet, as simple as these organisms were, they had more of a resemblance to a modern human than you might think. Much of the basic biochemistry of modern cells was already in operation 3.5 billion years ago, when organisms like modern blue-green algae grew in the waters of the earth. The earliest stages of evolution, then, produced organisms that share many of their properties with modern humans; that is, many of the chemical reactions in your cells are identical to those in primitive cells.

This state of affairs isn't really as surprising as it might appear at first glance. It fact, it is a straightforward consequence of the workings of natural selection, the process that drives all evolutionary change. You probably remember that natural selection works by preserving characteristics that give some organisms a better chance of surviving and reproducing than their neighbors. For example, suppose that by some chance an early cell had a slightly altered molecule that allowed it to run one of its chemical reactions more efficiently. You would expect, then, that this cell would get more out of the resources in its environment and would be more likely to reproduce itself and pass the gene for the altered molecule on to its descendants. These cells would also have a competitive edge, so they, too, would produce more offspring than the other members of their species. Over time, the proportion of cells in the population with the altered molecule would increase until, eventually, almost all the cells would have it. This is how organisms change to respond to their environment, and how, over geological time, new forms of life arise.

You can see that natural selection is not a process that can create new forms of life out of nothing. It can act only to alter forms of life that already exist. This fact leads to one of the great truths of biology: *All life comes from preexisting life*.

The evolution of life bears a striking resemblance to the development of a complex computer program. The program may start out as a relatively simple thing, but as the work proceeds you add pieces here and there to do new jobs. At each step, it is always easier to fiddle with the existing program than to go back and redesign from scratch. Eventually, you find that the program has become very complex. It works well but is nothing like the one you would write if you were starting to create one today. The program has evolved over time and carries within it the reminders of its past.

In precisely the same way all living things, descended from those earliest single-celled organisms, carry within them pieces of the simple "program" from which life started. This, in fact, is the reason that all life on earth is so similar biochemically.

The earliest single-celled organisms formed the base of the evolutionary tree. The first great branching took place when a new kind of organism appeared on the scene. Although the new organisms were single-celled, like their ancestors, their cells were highly structured and organized. Their DNA was no longer coiled in the body of the cell but contained in a nucleus. There were other structures in the cell, each designed to carry out specific tasks, such as the breaking down of food molecules, the production of energy, and the synthesis of chemicals. They were eukaryotes. The amoeba is an example of a single-celled eukaryote that exists today, and all of the cells in your body can be placed in this general category.

There is some controversy among scientists about when eukaryotes first appeared. Large cells of the type that might have had nuclei first show up in the fossil record from about two billion years ago. Some scientists who study the ways that DNA changes in evolutionary systems tend to think they showed up earlier, perhaps shortly after the prokaryotes them-selves. The most likely explanation for how the eukaryotes developed is this: At some point in the past, one prokaryote was totally engulfed by another. The two cells together enjoyed an advantage, and eventually the symbiosis became permanent. Evidence for this scenario comes from the fact that some struc-tures in a eukaryotic cell have two membranes around them: one presumed to be from the original cell, one from the cell that was absorbed.

For our purposes, the point to notice is that although we share our basic biochemistry with all life, prokaryotes and eu-karyotes alike, we share the property of having structured cells with nuclei only with eukaryotes. We do not, for example, share this property with modern bacteria and blue-green algae (cyanobacteria). This means that with the development of eu-karyotes, we can divide the realm of life and say, "This part is like us at the cellular level, and this part isn't."

Another important aspect of the appearance of eukaryotes is that a new kind of reproductive process became possible. Al-though single-celled organisms like the paramecium usually re-produce by a simple process of cell division, it occasionally happens that two paramecia come into contact and transfer a nucleus. This is an example of sexual reproduction. From the evolutionary point of view, sexual reproduction is extremely important because it produces and sustains a much wider diver-sity among offspring than does simple mutation. This diversity, in turn, gives natural selection more to work on and greatly increases the rate of evolutionary change.

The next major branching occurred between 600 and 700 million years ago, when single-celled organisms started to stay together to make more complex structures. At first, these multi-celled forms of life were probably just colonies of single cells living together — something like sponges today. Soon, however, the cells began to specialize and make use of division of labor, and true multicelled organisms came into existence. At first, they were soft-bodied things floating in the ocean (think of jellyfish), but around 590 million years ago hard parts and skeletons developed. We share the characteristic of multicellularity with other animals, with plants, and with some fungi.

But multicellularity creates problems never before faced by living systems, such as the problem of finding a method of communication between cells in different parts of the organism. The left hand, as it were, really has to know (and be able to respond to) what the right hand is doing. This need is particularly important in higher animals, where movement has to be orchestrated and controlled. The solution to this problem, of course, was the development of the nervous system.

At first, our animal ancestors were pretty unprepossessing things – small worms crawling around on the ocean bottom, with nervous systems consisting of only a few cells. Then, about 500 million years ago, another important branching occurred. Creatures appeared in which the problem of communication was solved by having a long strand of nerve fibers running down their backs, supported by a stiff rodlike structure. Called *chordates*, these animals possessed the start of a central nervous system. About 50 million years later, the nerve fibers were enclosed in a hollow bony tube of vertebrae – the first backbone. Humans share the property of having backbones with most of the living things, from fish to birds to elephants, that we normally think of when we hear the word *animal*, but this branching splits humans and their neighbors off from other animals such as insects, sponges, worms, and crabs, which are highly organized but have no spinal column.

The first primitive vertebrates, fish like the modern lamprey, served as ancestors for more advanced fishes and then, about 350 million years ago, for animals something like modern lungfish—fish that can breathe air for short periods of time. These part-time land dwellers developed into modern amphibians like frogs and salamanders, whose aquatic roots are evident in the fact that part of each individual's life cycle is spent in water, the remainder on land. We share the terrestrial lifestyle with amphibians and higher vertebrates, but this branching splits us off from fish and other purely aquatic life-forms.

Amphibians usually reproduce by depositing eggs and sperm in the environment simultaneously, perhaps with a jellylike substance that holds things together. Both fertilization and subsequent growth are left pretty much to chance (it is, in fact, the difficulty that sperm and egg would have coming together and developing on land that ties the amphibian to water for part of its life cycle). With the development of reptiles about 280 million years ago, animal life moved irrevocably to land. In reptiles, fertilization occurs inside the mother, the fertilized egg is surrounded by a tough protective shell, and the developing embryo is supplied with stored nourishment. Reptiles dominated life on earth until sixty-five million years ago, when a great cataclysm—probably the impact of a large asteroid—caused widespread devastation. Reptiles include the extinct dinosaurs as well as modern animals like snakes and lizards. They are also believed to be the ancestors of modern birds, so there is a link between *Tyrannosaurus rex* and your Thanksgiving turkey. With the reptiles we share a fully terrestrial lifestyle and a reproductive strategy that calls for protecting the embryo rather than leaving it totally to the mercies of the environment.

The reptiles that were the ancestors of modern mammals lived at about the same time as the ancestors of the dinosaurs. In fact, there were mammals (in the form of small shrewlike animals) around throughout the great age of reptiles. Mammals and birds, both descended from reptiles, are characterized by being warm-blooded. Their body temperature is determined by their internal physiological system, rather than by the temperature of the environment. They do not need to spend long periods sunning themselves before they can go about the business of food gathering and mating. Humans share warm-bloodedness with both birds and other mammals.

Mammals also developed more advanced means of nourishing and protecting the embryo. Although a few mammals, like the duck-billed platypus, lay eggs, and marsupials like the kangaroo and opossum carry their young in pouches after a short period in the uterus, the primary mammalian reproductive strategy involves allowing the entire development of the fetus to take place within the uterus. This process requires the development of a placenta, a structure found only in the most developed placental mammals, which appear in the fossil record 90 to 100 million years ago. We share the ability to give live birth with other placental mammals, but with this characteristic we split off from other mammals like the kangaroo and the platypus.

During the great development of mammals, a group of creatures something like modern lemurs arose. They had grasping fingers and toes, flat fingernails (instead of claws), and some other anatomical features (like having both eyes at the front of the head) that identify them as primates. They were the ancestors of modern monkeys, apes, and human beings.

The evolutionary tree from this point on becomes more and more specialized. As the early primates developed, the characteristics that separate them from each other (and from human beings) became more and more minute—the shape of a skull here, the cut of a tooth there. Somewhere along the line of primate evolution, there had to be a branching point that led, eventually, to modern humans.

This branch point happens to be in a period of time (five to ten million years ago) from which few data are available, so we don't have any detailed knowledge about it. We do know that there was a constellation of apelike animals that existed about ten million years ago, any one of which could have served as a common ancestor to humans and apes. A typical fossil from this group was discovered in Pakistan sixty years ago and named *Sivapithecus* ("Siva's ape"). This creature was about the size of a small chimpanzee. It had a narrow, orang-utanlike face and humanlike teeth but lacked the long arms of a tree swinger. It may or may not have been the last common ancestor of humans and the apes, but whatever that ancestor was, it probably had these sorts of mixed characteristics.

The animals that are often called the *first humans* (techni-cally, they are the first members of the hominid family) are a group of creatures whose fossils have been found in Ethiopia. The most famous of these fossils, a young female called Lucy by her discoverers, shows that the females weighed about sixty pounds—the males were presumably heavier—and that both probably resembled the modern chimpanzee in appearance. They differed from earlier primates in two crucial ways. First, they walked on two feet, so that their hands were freed for other uses, and second, they had larger brains. In fact, Lucy's adult companions had brains whose volume was about four hundred cubic centimeters, about the same size as the brain of a modern human at birth (and of a modern adult chimpanzee).

There were, of course, other features that distinguished Lucy from her fellows—the flatness of her face, the shape of her sinuses, and so on—but they were the sort of thing only experts would notice. For our purposes, the important fact about Lucy is that she represents a new departure in evolution. With the enlarging of the brain and, specifically, the enlarging of the outer layer of the brain, or cerebral cortex, a host of new possibilities opened. Eventually, this development would lead to the ability to make tools, to manipulate the environment, and even to reflect about oneself.

Again, we have to be careful about allowing hindsight to blur our picture of how evolution works. The cortex did not develop so that hominids could build airplanes and cathedrals. Most likely, it developed because the erect posture of early hominids gave an advantage to individuals with better hand–eye coordination than their neighbors. Once a slightly larger cortex was in place, its other possibilities, such as analytical ability, could be developed. This sort of unanticipated conse-quence is a common feature of evolution.

Lucy was a member of a species called *Australopithecus afar-ensis* ("southern ape from the Afar region of Ethiopia"). She was a member of the same family as human beings, but not the same genus or species. With her began a branch of the evolutionary tree whose only living representative is *Homo sapiens*. Thus, humans are separate from all other life-forms. Our quest for the quality of humanness, then, has to focus on what made Lucy and her descendants different.*

Lucy lived a little over three million years ago, and was followed by a series of other species of *Australopithecus*. Her descendants were larger and presumably more numerous and had brains in the range of four hundred to five hundred cubic centimeters as well. All australopithecines became extinct a little over a million years ago.

About two million years ago, the first member of the genus *Homo* appeared (also in Africa). *Homo habilis* ("man the tool-

---

*We use the term *descendants* loosely. The fossil record of human ancestors is too sparse for us to say with certainty that *A. afarensis* was a direct ancestor of modern humans. It could be that Lucy was on a side branch and we are descended from some equally ancient but as yet undiscovered group.

maker") had, as the name implies, the ability to use a variety of stone tools. They had a large brain (750 cubic centimeters) and were about the size of a modern twelve-year-old human child.

Homo habilis became extinct about 1.5 million years ago and was replaced in the fossil record by *Homo erectus*. Most of the famous fossils—Java man, Peking man, and so on—that you've heard of were of this type. *Homo erectus* was almost the size of modern humans, had a brain about two thirds the size of ours, and was the first of our ancestors to use fire. *Homo erectus* became extinct about a half million years ago.

This brings us to the very recent past, geologically speaking. People who looked pretty much like us—what scientists call *anatomically modern humans*—were walking around Africa 200,000 years ago. They were our ancestors and are the first appearance of *Homo sapiens* on the evolutionary tree. One hundred thousand years ago, another kind of human—the Neanderthal—was living in Europe and the Middle East.

Neanderthals were strong, heavy-boned people with a brain averaging some fifteen hundred cubic centimeters—somewhat larger than that of modern humans (see Table 3). They had fire and stone tools, of course, and also appear to have developed at least some aspects of advanced culture. They buried their dead with ceremony, for example, which argues for the existence of religious beliefs. They had the anatomical structures needed for human speech, and many scientists believe they had a language. They were, in all aspects we can measure, as "human" as it is possible to be.

There is a serious debate in the scientific community about whether the Neanderthals were simply a subspecies of *Homo sapiens*—as different from us as a St. Bernard is from a dachshund, for example—or whether they were a separate species altogether, as different from us as a dog is from a fox. It is our sense that the weight of the evidence at this time is starting to move in favor of the latter possibility. But separate species or not, we do know that Neanderthals in Europe disappeared suddenly thirty-five thousand years ago, about the time that modern humans (sometimes called *Cro-Magnons*) appeared on the scene. Whether this disappearance was the result of an early example of genocide or simply the displacement of one group by another—a process that occurs often in the fossil record—is also a subject of much debate.

With our ancestors from *Australopithecus* to the Neanderthal, modern humans share an ever-increasing brain capacity and hence an ever-increasing ability to invent technology. Thus we may propose a metaphor to help us think about how humans can be so similar and yet so different from other organisms. Adding the greatly enlarged cortex can be thought of as being similar to adding a hard disk to a computer. In both cases, most of the operating mechanism stays the same, but the sophistication is greatly enhanced.

Humanness

In Table 2, we summarize the important steps in the evolution of the modern human. In the last column, we list the extant living things with which humans share the trait developed at the time listed on the left. When we look at the table, the answer to our question about the nature of humanness is obvious. At each stage on the evolutionary tree, our ancestors shared new characteristics with a smaller and smaller group of organisms. Finally, at the very tip of our branch, we come to something that is shared by no other animals: the development of a large brain and, in particular, the development of a large cerebral cortex. And although there are other unshared characteristics (erect posture, for example), they clearly do not give

Table 2. *Steps in Evolution*

Time (million years)	Event	Characteristic	Shared With
3,600	First cell	Basic biochemistry	All life
2,000	Eukaryotes	Cell nucleus and other structures	Eukaryotes
700	Multicellularity	Complex organisms	Plants, fungi, animals
450	Vertebrates	Protected spinal chord	Fish, amphibians, reptiles, birds, and mammals
350	Amphibians	Part time on land	Amphibians, reptiles, birds, and mammals
280	Reptiles	Fully terrestrial, protected egg	Reptiles, birds, and mammals
100	Placental mammals	Warm-blooded, live birth	Placental mammals
65	Primates	Grasping hands	Primates
3-now	Lucy and other hominids, including *Homo sapiens*	Erect, large brain	None

us the fundamental separation from other species that we are looking for. A gorilla that is bipedal but like the familiar ape in all other respects would clearly not have the quality of humanness.

The development of brain size in our ancestors over the past three million years is summarized in Table 3. As the hominids evolved from Lucy to the present, there was a steady increase in brain size, with most members of *Australopithecus* already having brains significantly larger than those of present-day apes. We will discuss the complex relation between brain size and brain function in some detail in Chapter 6, but we present the

Table 3. *Brain Size of Hominids and Apes*

Animal	Brain Size (cubic centimeters)
Chimpanzee	400
Gorilla	500
Australopithecus afarensis (Lucy)	400
Australopithecus (later species)	450–500
Homo habilis	750
Homo erectus	900–1100
Neanderthals	1,500
Anatomically modern humans	1,400

data here to make our point about what it is that makes our particular twig on the tree of life different from all others.

The evolution of *Homo sapiens*, then, demonstrates unequivocally that there is an identifiable point at which we can say that evolving organisms acquired the quality of humanness. That stage occurred over three million years ago, when creatures appeared with enlarged cerebral cortices, and the process of expanding and exploiting the possibilities of this organ has been going on ever since.

The Moral Dilemma

One way to get at the specialness of our ancestors from Lucy on is to ask a simple question: Would most modern Americans consider it wrong to kill a member of a particular hominid species if that species were not extinct? Would we, in fact, call such an act *murder*, or would we view it the same way we view killing a great ape, as something to be avoided, but in no way analogous to killing another person in the present legal system?

There is little question in our mind that most modern humans would find the killing of a Neanderthal to be an immoral act. The Neanderthals, after all, were sufficiently like us so that there is a serious debate about whether to include them in *Homo sapiens*. We suspect that the same conclusion would be reached about *Homo erectus* and, probably, *Homo habilis*.

But what about the australopithecines? Would killing Lucy be different, morally, from killing a baboon or a chimpanzee? How far up the hominid tree do we have to go before we would use the word *murder*?

When we get into questions like this, we enter a kind of gray area—one where we feel uneasy about our ability to make moral judgments. Fortunately, none of these questions arise in daily life because none of these hominids is still around (perhaps because our own ancestors had fewer moral scruples in the matter than we think we would). These questions do, however, point out an inescapable property of debates about biological issues. There are few sharp distinctions among living systems—few clear boundaries. There are always gray areas, and we shouldn't be too surprised if we encounter more as our inquiry develops.

The Development of the Fetus

When the author of the Book of Psalms asked, "What is Man, that Thou art mindful of him?" (Psalms 8:4), we doubt very much that he would have anticipated an answer anything like that given by a twentieth-century biologist. In our discussion up to this point, two great truths have emerged about the place of humanity among living things. First, we have seen that at the level of individual cells (and, more important, at the level of individual molecules), human beings really aren't all that different from their relatives on the tree of life. We share a common genetic code, as well as a surprisingly high degree of overlap in the genetic messages, with organisms as different from us as pumpkins and brewer's yeast. Whatever it is that makes us unique and different, it is not to be found solely at this level.

The second great insight of modern biology concerns how life on our planet developed. We have seen that human beings are one product of an evolutionary process that goes back almost four billion years, to the formation of the first cell on our planet. It is only very recently (geologically speaking) that large-brained hominids like us appeared on the scene. Indeed, if you imagine the time since the appearance of that first cell as being compressed into one year, Lucy appeared on the scene just before sunset of New Year's Eve, and the first *Homo sapiens* less than a half hour before midnight.

This is why the analogy of the computer and the hard drive introduced in the last chapter is so important. The huge differences between human beings and other animals — differences obvious to even the casual observer — have arisen as a result of the addition of a greatly enlarged cerebral cortex to a quite ordinary primate. It is the functioning of this single structure that produces everything, from symphonies to supersonic aircraft, that differentiates us from the rest of the living world.

Identifying humanness with the cerebral cortex and its functions is not a particularly revolutionary (or even particularly original) proposition. Scientists and theologians have long put this view forward. Teilhard de Chardin, a Jesuit scholar, argued that humankind's transcendence hinged on the development of the cerebral cortex. Another Catholic theologian, Bernard Häring, argued in the 1970s that the cerebral cortex is the center of all personal manifestations and activities, and anatomist Paul Glees wrote in 1988 that "the [cerebral cortex] represents the signature of a genetically unique person."

Once we have made this identification, the task that remains is to ascertain the point at which each individual human acquires a functioning cerebral cortex, and therefore what we have called the *quality of humanness*. The best way to do this is to put the question in context, to look at how the human embryo and fetus develop during a pregnancy, and to ask ourselves at each step how much they have differentiated themselves from other forms of life and how much they still have in common with them.

Before beginning this discussion, we'd like to make one point very clear. We are going to present the story of the development of the individual fetus as a process that is in some ways analogous to the story of the historical evolution of human beings or to the tracing out of our position on the Linnean tree of life. We will, for example, look for the points when the fetus has acquired the properties of "vertebrate-ness" or "primate-ness." This approach provides us with a framework within which to discuss the very complex process of development, but there are pitfalls associated with it.

During the late nineteenth century, for example, there was a school of thought that carried this analogy to an untenable extreme. Operating under the slogan "Ontogeny (the development of an individual) recapitulates phylogeny (the development of a species)," it taught that each human fetus retraces the steps that our species followed in its evolution. The idea was that at one point in its development, the human fetus has the characteristics of an adult fish, later the characteristics of an adult amphibian, and so on. This notion is wrong, as we shall see. But like many ideas that are both wrong and interesting, this one contains more than a kernel of truth about the development of the fetus and evolution.

The First Month

We have already described how the nuclei of the sperm and the egg come together to form a full complement of DNA in the fertilized egg. At this point the machinery for producing the proteins that drive the cell's chemical reactions is in place.

Even at this first stage in development, the basic chemistry that we share with all other living things is present. Because the fertilized egg has its DNA in a nucleus, however, it already possesses the characteristics of a eukaryote; it has the properties we will call *eukaryote-ness*.

This means that in our loose analogy, we are skipping the first stages of the evolutionary process and beginning two billion years into the story. Although we share our basic chemistry with the prokaryotes, there is never any time in the development of a fetus when humans share the prokaryotes' structure.

With the first few cell divisions, we leave behind not only any resemblance to single-celled organisms, but resemblances to plants and fungi as well. As we pointed out in Chapter 3, a high level of plasticity is associated with the first few cell divisions in animals. In flowering plants, however, things don't work this way. After the sperm (carried in the pollen grain) fertilizes the egg, the first cell division produces descendants that are programmed to carry out different tasks. One of the offspring divides further to produce the structure analogous to the ovary, while the other produces a structure that ties the "ovary" to the outer coating of the seed. In effect, the first division of the zygote in a plant produces something like a miniature plant, while the first division in animals produces cells that can develop into any part of the adult organism.

It is an interesting historical fact that in the seventeenth century some scientists believed that a similar process occurred in humans. It was thought that each sperm contained a miniature adult human inside it, and that the function of the egg was to provide nourishment to let that adult grow.

The first few splittings of the human zygote, when it goes from 1 to 2 to 4 to 8 . . . cells, produces a ball of cells called the *blastula*. At this point, we have a system that resembles the early stages in development of all but the simplest animals. We can say that at this stage—typically three days into a pregnancy, when the trip down the Fallopian tube has yet to be completed—the developing system has acquired the quality of "animal-ness."

The resemblance of the human blastula to that of other animals is underscored by the fact that in the early years of this century, scientists who wanted to study the development of the blastula used sea urchins for their experimental animals. At this early stage of development, even the sea urchin—whose adults are about as different from us as an animal can be—isn't very different from a human being.

By the fourth day, further cell divisions have produced the beginnings of the blastocyst described in Chapter 3. This is also the time when the journey down the Fallopian tube is completed. By the sixth day, the blastocyst has implanted itself in the uterine wall. By the end of the first week, then, we have an embryo of some dozens of cells attached to the wall of the uterus.

During the next week, a complex set of cell divisions and differentiations take place, eventually turning the embryo into a flat, disklike structure about a sixteenth of an inch long. By the end of the second week, you can see an indentation, called the *primitive streak,* starting to form down the middle of the disk. By the eighteenth and nineteenth days, the streak has extended to form a groove from one end of the disk to the other. The cells along this groove will eventually house the nerves of the spine. This is the beginning of the central nervous system, and at this point in development we can say that the embryo has acquired the quality of "chordate-ness."

Along the groove, cells giving rise to structures called *somites* start to appear. They will eventually become the vertebrae that form the spinal column. By the end of the fourth week, there is a clear line of somites along what will be the backbone in the embryo, and in our language, we can say that it has acquired "vertebrate-ness." At this time, the beginnings of gut, liver, and heart can also be seen, and some blood cells are starting to form.

During this period, the human embryo bears a striking resemblance to those of other vertebrates, from fish to mammals. This resemblance is illustrated in Figure 3. It was this resemblance that gave rise to the "ontogeny recapitulates phylogeny" thesis mentioned above.

You can understand the sense in which the human embryo retraces the journey along the evolutionary pathway by looking at the gill-like structures in the embryo in the figure. These structures are called *pharyngeal arches* and can be seen in the embryos of all vertebrates. They look like primitive gills, and indeed, in fish they do eventually develop into gills. In the human, however, they never produce gills; instead, they grow to form parts of the head and neck. Just as evolution does not imply that humans descended from the apes but shared a common ancestor with them, the presence of pharyngeal arches does not imply that human and fish embryos both have gills, but only that they have parts that descended from the same primordial structure.

The Second Month

The second month is the period when most of the major organs of the human body start to form in the embryo. This is a period when the embryo is very susceptible to outside influences, and when many congenital malformations begin to be seen. The embryo at four weeks is still only a fraction of an inch long, but by the end of the second month, it has grown to a length of several inches. It has grown limbs with fingers and toes and a heart with the typical four-chambered structure of mammals. At two months, it is quite easy to tell the human embryo from that of a reptile, an amphibian, or a bird. It is during this period that the embryo acquires "mammal-ness."

During the second month, a series of changes begin to occur that give the embryo the distinctive features of the primates. The hands and feet of the embryo at five weeks are flat, plate-like structures at the ends of the arms and legs. Cells in the regions that will be the spaces between fingers and toes start to die off, so that the embryo is left with clearly defined hands and feet by the end of the seventh week.

At the end of four weeks, buds appear at the sides of the head and start to develop into eyes. This process takes a long time, and the eyes are not fully formed until much later in the pregnancy. During the second month, however, the developing eyes start to move toward the front of the head. (You will recall that having eyes in the front of the head, and the consequent acquisition of stereoscopic vision, is a distinguishing feature of primates.) By the end of the first trimester, then, the fetus has clearly acquired "primate-ness."

One point should be made very strongly at this juncture. By six weeks, the fetus is recognizably human in many features. It has a rudimentary face, limbs, fingers and toes, and so on. There is a temptation to think that it is therefore a complete human being in miniature, and that all that happens from this point on is that everything grows proportionately larger until birth. This impression is reinforced by standard drawings of fetal development, which show successively larger fetuses with the same outlines throughout the rest of the pregnancy.

The relative lack of change on the outside of the fetus is deceptive, however. Inside, where you can't see what's happening, an enormous amount of growth and change is going on.

FISH SALAMANDER TORTOISE

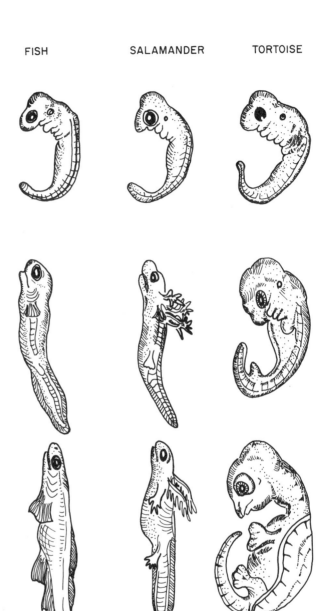

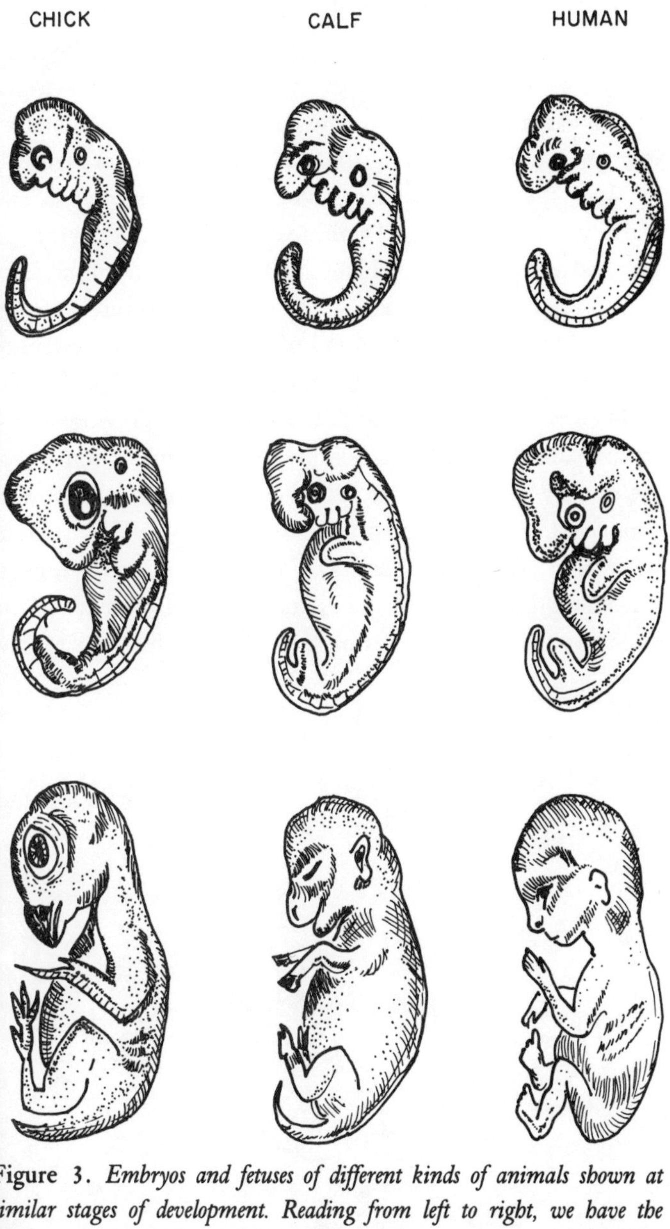

CHICK   CALF   HUMAN

Figure 3. *Embryos and fetuses of different kinds of animals shown at similar stages of development. Reading from left to right, we have the development of a fish, a salamander, a tortoise, a chicken, a calf, and a human being.*

In fact, as time goes by the main organs of the fetus—heart, gut, lungs, and so on—become more and more elaborated, more and more detailed in structure. For example, in Figure 4, we show the progressive development of the kidney at six and seven weeks and at birth. There are one to three million tubules that collect waste in the kidneys and deliver it to the bladder, and it simply takes time for all this detailed structure to form. We could show similar diagrams of any other organ system to make our point.

The best way to think of this type of organ development is to compare the fetus to a building under construction. Once the outer walls and roof are up, a building looks pretty much completed. In fact, there is an enormous amount of work to be done as electricians, plumbers, painters, and others convert the basic outline of the building into the final product. In the same way, the final two trimesters of pregnancy involve the

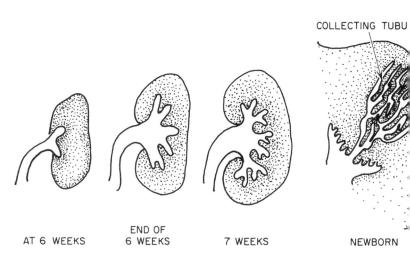

COLLECTING TUBU

AT 6 WEEKS   END OF 6 WEEKS   7 WEEKS   NEWBORN

Figure 4. *Development of kidneys.*

development of the fine structure of the internal organs of the fetus.

The Central Nervous System

We have not, as yet, found any aspects of the developing fetus that we can take as defining the quality of humanness. The weight of the arguments in Chapter 2 and Chapter 4 is that what distinguishes humans from other animals is to be found not in cellular chemistry or in physical structures, but in the structure and function of the brain. In order to understand how a fetus acquires humanness, then, we are going to have to go back and look at the development of the central nervous system and, in particular, the brain.

At twenty-two days, the embryo is about an eighth of an inch long and bears a striking resemblance to a corncob (see Figure 5). The "kernels" are the somites (see page 90) that will eventually develop into vertebrae. At the top are some flange-like structures around an opening that leads to the interior of the "corncob," a hollow region known as the *neural tube*.

By the fourth week, the neural tube has closed off, and the cells that line it near the top have grown to form a curved structure (see Figure 6) that is the beginning of the nervous system and the brain. At this stage of development the nervous system of a human and that of a chicken are pretty much the same. In fact, at this stage we would say that the embryo has achieved "vertebrate-ness" as far as its nervous system is concerned but has progressed no further.

Various parts of the curved structure develop into different parts of the fetus. Even at four weeks, for example, there is a small bulge at the forward part of the curve. These are the cells that will eventually develop into eyes. Cells far down on

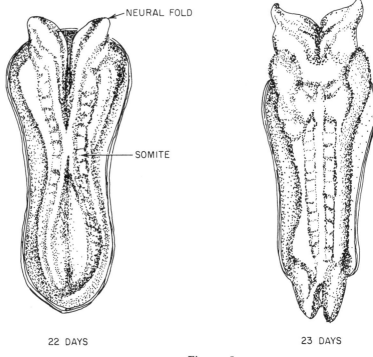

22 DAYS   23 DAYS

Figure 5

the right-hand portion of the curve (those that were inside the hollow tube described above) will develop into a primitive spinal cord and then grow branches that will eventually become a web of nerves that communicates to all parts of the body. The rest of the top and left-hand side of the curve is what develops into the brain.

This is a story best told in pictures. In Figure 6 we see the development of the brain at intervals from three and one-half weeks until birth. At seven weeks, the eye bud is easy to see, and the various bumps and wiggles in the embryo mark places where divisions between different parts of the brain will occur later. At this point, however, the human embryo and those of

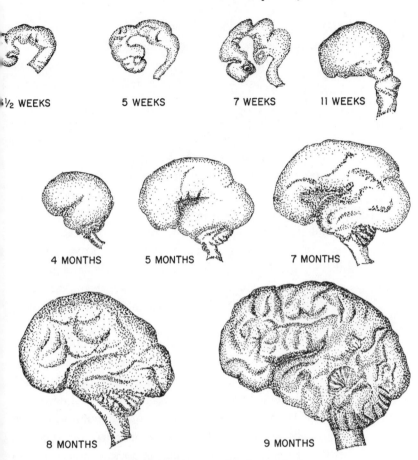

Figure 6. *Development of the human brain.*

other vertebrates would still bear a striking resemblance to each other.

By eleven weeks, however, the situation has changed. As we shall see in a moment, the embryonic brain is now clearly recognizable as mammalian. The large lump in front is what will eventually grow into the cerebral cortex—the structure whose function we wish to identify with the property of humanness. A glance at the succeeding sketches shows that at eleven weeks the broad outlines of the familiar human brain are already in place, although a great deal of elaboration is still to come.

These diagrams illustrate some general rules of development in the nervous system. First, the general scheme is that cells migrate to a region, come together to make the basic outlines of large structures, and then mature and differentiate to put the structure in its final form. Building the brain, in other words, is like building a house. First, the general structure is assembled—the walls are raised, the roof completed, and so on. Only after this work has been finished do we go on to filling in the details. The brain simply does not develop so that at some point you have half a complete organ, then three fourths, and so on. The brain isn't completed until the finishing work is done.

The second point, related to the first, is that once the gross structure is in place, most of the action takes place at the level of the cells and is not visible to the naked eye. So important is the cellular development of the brain that we will devote the entire next chapter to discussing it. For the moment, though, we simply note that the fact that the brain has something like its final appearance at four months in no way implies that the four-month brain is anything like a full-term brain in terms of how it works and what it can do.

While the diagrams in Figure 6 show the development of a single human brain very clearly, they offer no information about how or when that development produces a brain that is different from those of other animals. To understand this aspect of nervous system development, it will be necessary to stop for a few moments and review the structure and functioning of the adult human brain.

The Brain

A cross section of the human brain is shown in Figure 7. Although the brain is an organ of extraordinary complexity, we can make a rough division by breaking it into three parts: the hindbrain, the midbrain, and the forebrain. Let's look at each of these separately.

The hindbrain is located at the base of the brain, where the spinal cord comes in. It is made up of three major organs: the medulla and the pons, which are essentially a thickening of the spinal cord itself, and the cerebellum, which grows out of the back of the spinal cord. Each of these organs plays a role in controlling basic body functions. The medulla, for example, controls breathing and plays an important role in regulating blood pressure and the functions of the intestine. These are functions that proceed without conscious thought, but that are essential in the maintenance of the body. Similarly, the cerebellum keeps track of the state of the body and modifies posture and movements in accordance with this information. For example, if you were to put this book down, the command to your arm muscles would arise in parts of the brain other than the cerebellum. As your arm moved, however, small corrections would have to be made in the muscles in your back and legs for you to maintain your balance. You don't think about these small corrections; they just happen automatically. This sort of automatic posture control is a function of the cerebellum. The familiar test in which a doctor asks you to touch the tip of your nose with your eyes closed is designed to test the functioning of the cerebellum.

The pons (the term is the latin word for "bridge") forms a connection between the medulla and the cerebellum and seems to play an important role in passing information between the cerebrum (where conscious action arises) and the cerebellum.

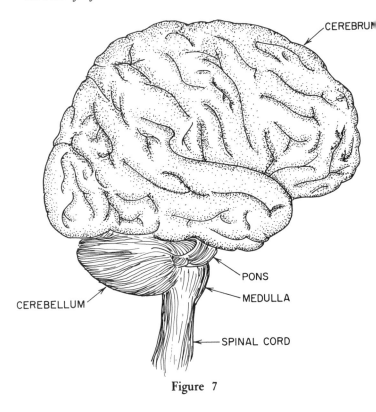

CEREBRUM

PONS

MEDULLA

CEREBELLUM

SPINAL CORD

Figure 7

The pons seems to be particularly important in things like walking and hand–eye coordination, which require a lot of posture control and compensation, and it is therefore particularly important in primates.

The midbrain is a thickening at the end of the spinal column. The midbrain controls the movement of the eye, and in lower vertebrates, the midbrain is where visual information is processed. In mammals, this processing is done higher up in the brain, but the midbrain is used to process information from the ears.

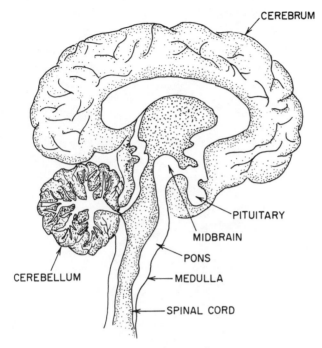

Figure 7 *(continued)*

The midbrain and the hindbrain are often referred to collectively as the *brain stem;* they do have the appearance of a pedestal on which the forebrain is placed. As you can see, the brain stem regulates the basic body functions. All vertebrates have this much structure in their brains; for example, in Figure 8 we show the brain of an adult fish. This brain is almost all stem, with very little additional structure. We can speak, then, of the brain stem as being part of the "vertebrate-ness" of the human being—as something we share with all vertebrates.

The forebrain is the part of the brain that overlays the stem. When you look at the human brain, you normally see only the forebrain, since it is by far the largest part. Although the

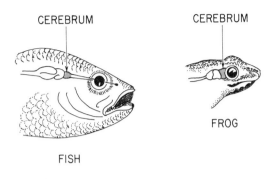

FISH

FROG

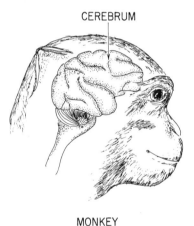

MONKEY

Figure 8

forebrain is itself a fairly complex structure, we will think of it as divided roughly into two parts. The lowest part, just above the brain stem, is called the *diencephalon*. It contains a region called the *thalamus*, which serves as a relay station for sensory information on its way to higher parts of the brain, and a region called the *hypothalamus*, which controls basic body metabolism. The hypothalamus controls the pituitary gland, among other things, and is in charge of the hormonal balance of the body. For example, it controls a woman's menstrual cycle.

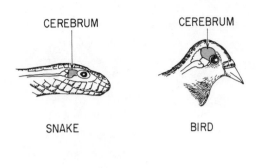

CEREBRUM

CEREBRUM

SNAKE

BIRD

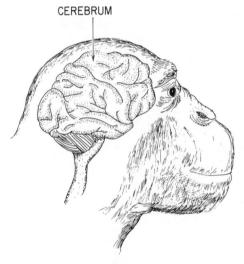

CEREBRUM

CHIMPANZEE

Figure 8 *(continued)*

The remainder of the forebrain consists of the two lobes of the cerebrum, the "gray matter" we normally picture when we think of the brain. The lower cortex—the parts near the thalamus and the hypothalamus—governs functions like smelling. There is also a complex of tissue known as the *limbic system* that lies partly in the lower cerebrum and partly in the diencephalon that governs visceral emotions such as anger, fear,

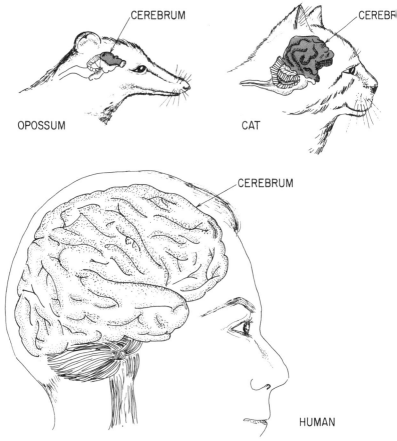

OPOSSUM CAT

CEREBRUM CEREBR

CEREBRUM

HUMAN

Figure 8 *(continued)*

sexual arousal, and feeding behavior. We share these systems with other vertebrates.

The outer layer of the cerebrum, the wrinkled, convoluted cerebral cortex, is what will occupy most of our attention throughout the rest of the book, for it is here that the properties that distinguish human beings from other animals are ultimately found to reside. In the human brain, specific areas of the cerebral cortex are involved in speech, conscious movement, the processing of visual information, taste, and other sensory information from different parts of the body. The complex functions that we associate with human beings, such as social interactions and intellectual endeavor, are located in the front lobe.

The things we call *mind* and *consciousness* are clearly associated with the brain, and particularly with the cerebral cortex. In his textbook on physiological psychology (see the bibliography), Richard Thompson says:

> Severe brain damage can reduce a person to a reflex machine that shows no sign of consciousness or mind. Damage limited only to the cerebral cortex, the highest region of the brain, appears to abolish completely all human characteristics, abilities, and awareness.

The Meaning of Brain Structure and Development

The standard division of the brain into hind-, mid-, and forebrain gives us a simple way to look at its structure and function. There is, however, a danger of oversimplification here. As the example of the limbic system shows, parts of the brain from these different divisions can and do interact with each other in a complex way. Nevertheless, the brain does have the general feature that as we move up from the brain stem to the frontal lobe of the cortex, we encounter areas concerned with progressively higher functions.

Our discussion of brain development in the embryo, however, shows that it is not a simple matter of adding ever more complex layers to the basic reptilian brain stem. In fact, all three regions of the brain develop together, and the cells that will give rise to all of them are clearly visible in the four-week embryo. Nor is it true that only higher vertebrates have brains with a cerebrum; even fish have them.

What distinguishes the human brain from the brains of other animals, then, is not that a totally new structure has been added, but that an old structure has grown and elaborated to the point where it has acquired new and unexpected functions. As we move up through the vertebrates, we find brains in which a greater and greater fraction of the weight is taken up by the cerebral cortex, until in humans it reaches 70 percent. This is shown clearly in Figure 8.

Humans are different not because they have a cortex, then, but because they have a big cortex. Something qualitatively different happens when the cortex gets to a certain size—something that only human beings have so far attained. In the language of biologists and engineers, the distinctly human functions of the cortex are an emergent feature of brain development.

There are many examples of situations in which complex systems are more than the sum of their parts. A city of a million inhabitants, for example, is more than just one hundred towns of 10,000 laid down side by side. The city has features that the towns do not, such as symphony orchestras, coffee shops, and specialty stores of all kinds. When a human population reaches a certain size, new kinds of organizations emerge that weren't there before. In the same way, the human cortex is not just a few thousand alligator cortices tied together, but something totally new.

Every animal has to have a part of its brain that regulates breathing and controls basic metabolism. We share the functions of the brain stem and the diencephalon with all other animals. Even in the cerebral cortex, we find functions like motor control and interpretation of vision—functions we also share with other animals. But in part of the cortex, we find something that we don't share with other species. From the frontal lobe, the seat of higher functions, come the things that make human beings different from other animals. When we put up a cathedral, write a symphony, or even just take part in simple social interactions, it is this part of the brain that is involved.

The study of the respective brain structures of different species, then, leads us to the same conclusion as the study of human evolution: Humanness is tied to the development of the cerebral cortex. But when does the cortex develop in an individual? Is it at four weeks, when the first lumps appear on the curved structure? Is it at seven weeks, when the first cells that will eventually be part of the cortex are made and begin migrating to their final position? Is it at some point in the final months, when the cortex begins to attain its final size and configuration?

So long as we confine our attention to the large-scale features of the developing brain—what scientists call its *gross anatomy*—this question simply cannot be answered. The development of the brain is a smooth continuum, with no place where sharp distinctions can be drawn. If we look at what is going on *inside* the developing brain, however, the story is quite different. We will find that at the level of the cells, there are relatively sharp boundaries in time, and that it is relatively easy to match these boundaries to the onset of meaningful changes in brain function. It is at the level of the individual cells and their connections, then, that we will find the answer to our quest for humanness.

6

The Birth of
the Cortex

Like everything else in the human body, the brain and the cortex are made of cells. The working components of the brain are specialized nerve cells, similar to the cells that make up the rest of the nervous system. Nerve cells are distinguished by their ability to transmit nerve impulses along individual cells and from one cell to another.

But the brain is not just a collection of cells, any more than a building is just a pile of bricks. Bricks have to be assembled and connected to each other to make a building, and the nerve cells in the brain have to be connected to make the system function. We have argued that the acquisition of humanness in the fetus is linked to the development of the cerebral cortex. The question of when the cortex develops, however, really involves two separate processes. One is the growth of the cells that make up the brain, the other is the establishment of the connections between them. Only when both of these tasks have been completed will we be able to say that the fetus has acquired those properties that distinguish human beings from everything else in the web of life.

A great deal of research on the development of connections in the cortex has been done since *Roe v. Wade*. We'll describe this work in a moment, but the bottom line is this: There appears to be a well-defined period in the third trimester of pregnancy when the great majority of connections between nerve cells in the cortex are made. It is this period that we propose to identify with what we have called the *acquisition of humanness*.

Since this conclusion is the most crucial element in our argument, it is a good idea to look a bit more closely at the way nerve cells are built, how they work, and how they go about connecting to one another.

The Nerve Cell

The basic structure of the nerve cell is shown in Figure 9. The cell has a main body (where the nucleus is located) with a

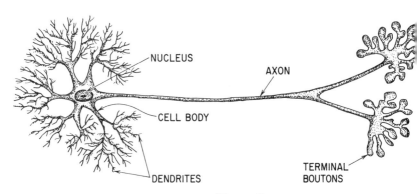

Figure 9

number of long filamentlike structures going out from it. The most prominent of these is a long tubelike structure called the *axon*. Think of it as a kind of telegraph wire that carries signals quickly over long distances. Although nerve cells are microscopic things, the axons may be surprisingly long—up to three feet in some human cells. There are, for example, axons that extend from your brain stem down to the small of your back. The axon typically has many branches, each ending in a buttonlike structure called a *terminal bouton* (the word is French for "button"). It is the boutons that transmit the nerve signals to other nerve cells, and each bouton can, in principle, make a connection with a different neighbor. Just as the main trunk on a telegraph line can split and hook up to many terminals, so, too, can a single nerve cell send out messages that influence many other cells.

In addition, there are branching, filamentary structure coming out of the cell body. These are called *dendrites* (from the Greek word for "tree"). In mature cells, the dendrites often have numerous small sideshoots, called *spines*, growing from them. The dendrites, as well as the cell body itself, are places where the nerve receives signals from surrounding cells.

There is, then, a simple picture of the ways nerve cells connect with each other. Each cell takes in information primarily through the dendrites and the cell membranes and sends out information primarily through the axon and the terminal boutons.

It is tempting to think of the nerve signals traveling along the axon as being something like the electrical current running through the wires in your house. As it turns out, the two have little in common except that both involve electricity. In your household wires, the current is composed of electrons that have been released by atoms and are being pushed through the wires. Signals traveling along an axon are much more complex.

For completeness, we are going to discuss what nerve signals are and how nerve cells communicate with each other. Readers not wishing this degree of detail may, if they wish, skip ahead to the section titled "The Assembling of the Brain" on page 113.

The outer membrane of the nerve cell is a pretty complex structure. It's not a solid sheet, like a balloon, but has all sorts of microscopic channels in it. Charged atoms and molecules can move through these channels, either to enter or to leave the cell. Depending on the size and shape of the channels (as well as some more complex factors), different charged atoms and molecules can move through them. In essence, there is one type of channel suited to each kind of material that has to pass through the membrane.

If you take a piece of ordinary table salt and drop it into a glass of water, the sodium and chlorine atoms of which the salt is made will break loose from the crystal of salt and diffuse through the water. The chlorine will have an extra electron (you can think of this as an electron that the chlorine took from the sodium when the crystal formed). Thus the chlorine will have a negative electrical charge (because of the extra negative electron), and the sodium will have a positive charge (because it is missing an electron). Atoms that have too many or too few electrons are called *ions*.

In the region of a resting axon, four kinds of things carry electrical charges. There are sodium and chlorine ions of the type we've just described, potassium ions (which, like sodium, have lost one electron and are therefore positively charged), and some molecules (including proteins) that have picked up or lost electrons. Sodium ions are concentrated outside the axon; chlorine ions and negatively charged molecules, inside. In the normal state, only the potassium channels in the membrane are open, so positively charged potassium ions tend to migrate out of the cell. The result is that there are positive charges outside the membrane and negative charges inside.

Whenever charges are separated this way, energy is stored in the system. It is, for example, the same sort of separation of charges between the plates of a battery that supplies the energy to start your car in the morning, or that runs your flashlight.* We usually measure the strength of a battery in terms of its voltage: a car battery is typically 12 volts, a flashlight battery 1.5 volts. The voltage across the membrane of a nerve cell is seventy thousandths of a volt—about one thirtieth of the voltage across the contacts of a flashlight battery. It is this energy, ultimately, that accounts for the ability of the cell to transmit signals.

Before we explain how this happens, however, we should make one point. Although we have been describing everything in terms of nerve cells, every living cell in the human body (and in the world, for that matter) has some sort of electrical energy at its surface. Even some structures inside the cells (such as those known as *mitochondria*) have voltages across the membranes that surround them. Life is intimately connected with electricity, right down to the simplest single-celled prokaryote.

What distinguishes a nerve cell, then, is not the fact that it has electrical activity at its surface, but the fact that it has the ability to change the arrangements of charges quickly (this property is shared by some muscle cells as well).

Here's how the nerve cell works: When an electrical stimulus is applied to the axon, the membrane changes. If the stimulus is past a certain threshold, positive sodium ions start to enter the interior rapidly. The result is that the voltage across the membrane drops (in effect, the "battery" is discharged), and

---

*The expert will realize that the membrane is more analogous to a charged capacitor than to a battery.

because there is so much more sodium outside the membrane than inside, the voltage actually reverses, so that the inside is more positive than the outside. As soon as this happens, the sodium stops entering and the potassium channels open. Positive potassium ions move out through the membrane and restore the initial equilibrium.

This entire operation (which goes by the name of *action potential*) takes place in somewhat less than a thousandth of a second. The nerve signal consists of a pulse moving down the axon, sodium pouring in at the front, and potassium moving out at the back. It is a complex motion of ions across the cell membrane, not a simple flow of charged particles down a wire as in an ordinary electrical current.

Although there is a rapid change in voltage when the action potential moves by a point on the axon, the number of charges that move across the membrane isn't all that great. Only a small percentage of the sodium (or potassium) ions move for one pulse. This means that the axon can carry repeated signals without having to restore all the charges to their original positions (although there is a short period after the passage of the pulse when the membrane cannot transmit signals). Eventually, after all the signals have passed, some of the cell's energy has to be used to pump all the ions back—to recharge the battery, as it were.

One important aspect of the way a nerve signal is generated is that it is an all-or-nothing affair. If the original stimulus is too small to remove the sodium barrier, nothing will happen. If it is large enough to do so, then the rest of the process is automatic and does not depend on the stimulus at all. The standard analogy is with the firing of a rifle. When the trigger is squeezed, there is either enough force to produce a shot or there isn't. Once there is the requisite force to pull the trigger back, however, the rest of the process depends only on the design of the rifle. The speed of the bullet, for example, doesn't depend on how hard you pull on the trigger. This fact about nerve signals is incorporated into the jargon of people who study them: they speak of the nerve "firing" when the signal starts.

In the brain, a typical cell receives signals from up to a thousand other cells. As we will see in a moment, each of these signals can move the cell to fire or not to fire. At any given moment, the nerve cell performs a complex operation that involves integrating all the signals it is receiving and comes to a single decision: it either fires or it doesn't. In this sense, then, each neuron in the brain can be thought of as a small computer, analyzing information and producing an output. The question of how the nerve cell goes about making its decision is one of the major research areas in neurophysiology today.

In some nerve cells, there is a bit of sophistication added to the propagation of signals down an axon. As the nerve cell matures, specialized neighboring cells wrap themselves around the axon, coating it with an insulating layer called *myelin*. There are gaps in the layer every so often, and the nerve signal, which can't travel through the insulation, has to jump from one gap to the next. This increases the speed of the signal considerably—to more than 250 miles per hour in some cases.

A signal moving down an axon eventually reaches the branchings at the end and arrives at the terminal boutons. Like a traveler encountering a raised drawbridge, the signal finds its progress halted by the existence of an uncrossable gap, a space a few hundred atoms wide that separates the bouton from the next nerve cell. What happens to a nerve signal when it encounters this gap? How are signals transmitted from one nerve cell to another?

The signal does not jump the gap the way an ordinary electrical spark jumps from one place to the next. Instead, when the signal arrives at the bouton, special molecules, called *neurotransmitters*, are released from little sacs there. The molecules diffuse across the gap just as molecules of perfume diffuse through the air in a room. When the neurotransmitters arrive at the other side of the gap, they find molecules in the surface that are shaped so that they fit exactly. They lock in, and their arrival starts another signal moving through the next cell. There are over twenty known neurotransmitters, some of which seem to excite an action potential in the receiving cell, and some of which inhibit that signal.

The gap between the bouton and the neighboring cell, together with the two membranes that define its boundaries, is called a *synapse*. Synapses are what form the overwhelming number of connections between nerves. Since the functions of the brain depend almost exclusively on the ability of nerve cells to communicate with each other, synapses are also key to understanding the brain.

Before going into the role of synapses in the brain in more detail, however, we should discuss the materials that alter the functioning of the synapses described above. Narcotics like heroin and morphine, for example, consist of molecules that are just the right shape to bind to the spot where neurotransmitters are usually received, and thus they have the effect of blocking the nerve signal. This is why morphine is widely used as a painkiller.

The famous South American poison curare blocks the transmission of the nerve impulse from nerve to muscle and produces paralysis (eventually stopping the breathing), but it does not affect the incoming signals from the sensory organs. Curare was originally found in vines, where it seems to have functioned as a natural insecticide. It produces effects quite similar to the illness myasthenia gravis, and it figured prominently in early research on that disease. We should note in passing, however, that the fact that a natural insecticide found in a South American vine can produce paralysis in virtually all advanced life-forms tells us that the basic chemistry of neurotransmission, like the basic chemistry of the cell, is shared by all complex animals.

The Assembling of the Brain

The cells that will eventually be part of the cerebral cortex begin forming in the seven-week embryo. They are originally in the form of primitive cells that have no axons or dendrites. They migrate to positions in what will eventually be the cortex, where they build up in layers, with the earliest arriving cells at the bottom. Throughout the development of the fetus, the brain grows in size, as you can see by looking at Figure 10.

Once in place, the cells start to mature, growing axons and dendrites in the process. All the primitive cells do not develop in the same way, however. Depending on where they are in the cortex, they will develop into one of six types of cells. These six types of cells constitute six distinct layers in the cortex, as is shown in Figure 11. Even at this early stage of development, then, the brain cannot be thought of as something that is simply a collection of nerve cells. It has a highly complex structure, and it would not function if that structure were not present.

We should also point out that nerve cells are not the only cells to be found in the brain. Fully 90 percent of the cells there are not nerve cells, but a different type called a *glial cell*. It used to be thought that their function was similar to that of tissue paper in packing a box—that they provided the support

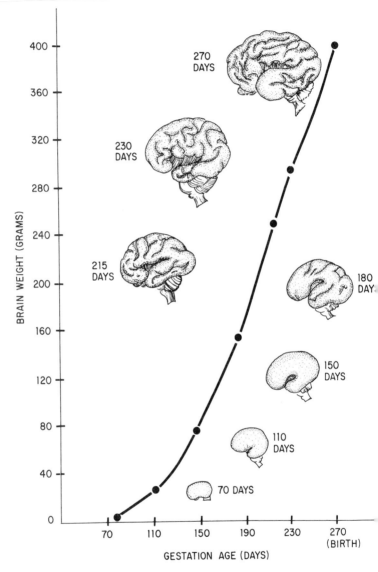

Figure 10

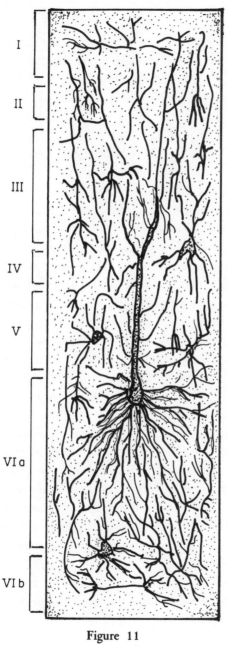

Figure 11

structure on which the nerve cells rest. The glial cells do perform this function, but recent research has shown that they also exchange nutrients with the nerve cells and seem to be generally involved with their care and feeding.

How the Brain Wires Itself

A pile of wires and switches is not an electrical circuit. A pile of microchips is not a computer. In the same sense, a collection of nerve cells, even nerve cells fully equipped with axons and dendrites, is not a functioning brain. The wires and microchips need to be connected to make the circuit or computer, and the nerve cells in the cortex need to be connected before we can say that we have a functioning brain. And since we have identified the quality of humanness with the functions of the cortex, it follows that we cannot say that the fetus has acquired this quality until the nerve cells have been connected, that is, until the brain has been "wired up."

Given what we know about the way that nerve signals are transmitted, then, the question of when the fetus acquires humanness (which we have, you will recall, related to the presence of the cerebral cortex) comes down to this: When do nerve cells in the brain form synapses?

Before synapses are formed, the fetal brain is just a collection of nerve cells. The fetus is incapable of awareness or volition. After the synapses have formed, the brain is functional. The time of the formation of synapses, then, becomes the key issue in our inquiry.

There are two sources of information on this question. One is the study of brain tissue obtained in autopsies of stillborn or prematurely delivered infants. The other is in studies of fetal brain tissue from monkeys and other primates. In both cases, thin slices of brain tissue are examined with an electron microscope, and the number and types of synapses are counted. By comparing the number from brains at different stages of development, one can, in effect, see the wiring as it proceeds.

The most extensive data are on the development of synapses in the rhesus monkey. Some twenty-two cortices were examined, a task that involved analyzing over twenty-five thousand pictures. We can summarize the finding in two statements: (1) The number of synapses from all parts of the cortex seem to increase at about the same rate (that is, we do not have a situation where synapses are connected first in one region, then another), and (2) although a few synapses are formed early in the pregnancy, the serious business of wiring up the brain in monkeys doesn't begin until a time that would correspond to about twenty-one weeks in human gestation.

Figure 12 is a graph showing typical data about the number of completed synapses in one region of the brain of rhesus monkeys. Notice the sharp upturn at 100 days (about 150 days in the human equivalent).

What this result gives us is a rather simple picture of the development of the cortex. Most brain cells are produced early in the pregnancy, migrate to their final position, and mature into their final form. During this period, a few synapses form, but there is no large-scale wiring up. Then, when most of the cells are in place and all is in readiness, synapses start forming in earnest. It is this burst of synapse formation that we call the birth of the cerebral cortex. It marks the period during which the brain is transformed from a collection of individual cells into a connected machine capable of carrying out human thought.

This picture is borne out by studies on human brain tissue.

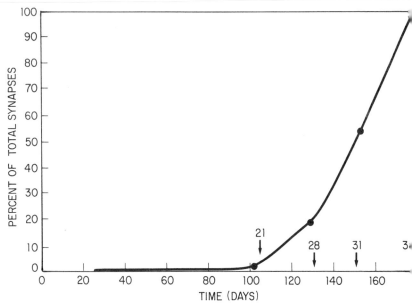

Figure 12. *The formation of synapses in the cortex of rhesus monkeys. The data adapted from the work of Rakic et al. (see the bibliography). In converting synapse density total number, we have assumed an increase of volume by a factor of 5 over the final eig days of pregnancy and normalized to the total number at full term. The numbers arrows indicate equivalent human gestation in weeks.*

Once again, we have a situation in which cells migrate into place, mature, and then start making connections. As a general rule, embryologists reckon that cells grow and migrate from Months 2 to 5, differentiate and form the cortex structure shown in Figure 10 in Month 6, and form large numbers of synapses starting in Month 7.

In humans, in fact, studies have shown that the connections in the visual cortex start being made at about twenty-five weeks. According to Dominic Purpura, Dean of the Albert Einstein College of Medicine in New York and the author of the major study in this field, by eight months the visual cortex (the part of the brain he studied) is physiologically equivalent to that of a full-term infant (see the bibliography). This result, together with the finding from the monkey studies that synapses in all parts of the brain form at the same time, leads to a picture for humans in which there is a period between twenty-five and thirty-two weeks when the cortex is coming into existence as a functional entity. During the last few weeks of this period (roughly from twenty-eight to thirty-three weeks in the pregnancy), there is a spurt of growth of spines on the dendrites, which greatly increases the area on which synapses may form.

A similar picture emerges when we look at the process of adding myelin to nerve axons in the brain. Although there is some myelination during the second trimester, the rate at which it is added begins to increase rapidly during the third trimester, starting earliest in the brain stem (where significant myelination can be seen starting at twenty-four weeks) and moving up to the cerebral cortex (where many parts do not show significant myelination even at birth). The greatest burst of myelination takes place after birth and isn't completed until after the first decade of life.

The period from twenty-five to thirty-two weeks, then, is what we will identify as the time during which the fetus acquires the property of humanness.

Before we go on to consider the consequences of this statement, there are several points we would like to make. First, the formation of synapses may start at a fairly well-specified time during the pregnancy, but it does not end at birth. In fact, in both humans and monkeys, synapses continue to form during infancy and early childhood. After birth, the human brain typically increases threefold in size, and the density of the synapses continues to increase for a few years, after which it drops and reaches a stable number. Roughly speaking, a person enters adulthood with about the same density of synapses in the brain as were present at birth, although the post-birth increase in size means that an adult has more synapses than a child. In any case, from the point of view of brain development, birth is not a singular event in the life of the individual.

The second point we want to make is that each nerve cell in the brain forms a large number of connections to other cells. Typically, there are a thousand terminal boutons on each cell, connecting that cell to other cells in the brain. Each cell is, in addition, able to receive signals from up to a thousand other cells (not necessarily the same ones to which it transmits). Thus the brain is interconnected to a degree that is almost impossible for us to comprehend. There are about 100 billion cells in the brain – about the same number as there are stars in the Milky Way. This means that the "wiring diagram" of the brain must have *100 trillion* synaptic connections. Considered in purely mathematical terms, brain wiring is more complex a problem than any other humans have ever thought of solving.

This fact, incidentally, probably explains why it is that we have not been able to build computers that function as the human mind does. It used to be thought that, since each neuron either fires or doesn't fire, it could be compared to a switch that is either on or off, and hence as carrying one bit of information. In computers, the on-off switch is a transistor, and people felt that if they could just build a computer with enough transistors in it, they would have something that was in some way the equivalent of the brain.

The problem is that transistors in computers are typically connected to only a few others; there is nothing like the degree of connectedness found in the brain. Perhaps this is why experts in artificial intelligence seem to be concentrating on putting together programs that mimic the observed operation of the brain.

Electrical Activity in the Brain

We often associate activity in the brain with the electroencephalogram (EEG). Indeed, the absence of an EEG signal is now accepted as a legal definition of brain death in patients being kept alive by life support systems in hospitals. A great deal has been written about fetal EEGs, so it is appropriate to discuss them in the context of the birth of the cortex.

Operationally, nothing could be simpler than taking an EEG. Electrodes are attached to different places on the subject's skull, and the voltage between the two is measured. Over time, the voltage changes. If it is plotted on a piece of graph paper, it goes up and down to produce the familiar "brain waves." Several different frequencies characterize the time it takes for the voltage to go up and down, from the eight to twelve times per second of the so-called alpha rhythm (characteristic of deep sleep) to the five to seven times per second of the theta rhythm characteristic of extreme stress. Over the years, scientists have learned to recognize different patterns in the oscillating voltage, and it is now easy to pick out the various rhythms that characterize different mental states. This can be done even though we don't have a clear idea of how the EEG patterns we see are related to the basic process of nerve cell activity in the brain.

The point is that the EEG represents a kind of organized electrical activity in the brain, an activity that must be related in some as yet unknown way to the actions of individual neurons. The EEG is one of those measurements that is very easy to make, but extremely difficult to interpret in any fundamental way.

The electrical activity of a mature brain produces signals that are easily recognizable. The question, of course, is when such patterns appear in the fetus. Even though we don't know what the connection between neural activity and the EEG is, we would certainly want to argue that when recognizable, organized EEGs appear, the fetus is starting to show the kind of mental activity that we associate with the quality of humanness.

EEG data cannot be gathered *in utero*. How could you get in to attach the electrodes? Instead, EEGs are taken on premature infants. In general, what is found is this: At twenty-five weeks, about the time that the synapses start forming, bursts of recognizable signals start to appear in the EEG, interspersed with periods of signals that are more-or-less random. The closer to birth we get, the more the recognizable patterns start to dominate the EEG until, at thirty-two weeks, the signals are essentially the same as those of a full-term infant. Like synapse formation, the EEG continues to change after birth and doesn't settle down into adult patterns until the child reaches the age of ten.

For our purposes, a good summary of the data on the onset of the EEG is given by Donald Scott in his book *Understanding the EEG* (see the bibliography): "Attempts have been made to record cerebral activity of premature infants and they have succeeded (only) if the gestational age was 25 weeks or more."

One claim that is often made in the abortion debate (by those arguing both sides of the issue) is that the fetal brain exhibits "electrical activity" at some astonishingly early age. We have seen claims in which this age ranges from nine to twelve weeks. For example, the following quotation is taken from an article about the philosophical aspects of the abortion controversy by Goldenring in the scholarly *Journal of Medical Ethics*: "If the fetus has reached the age of 8 weeks, a wealth of evidence indicates that its brain has begun functioning electrically."

Given what we know about the way the brain is formed, this sort of claim just didn't make sense to us, regardless of the fact that it seems to be widely accepted. We decided to try to track down the original data from which the claim comes. The result of this bit of detective work constitutes, we think, a cautionary tale about how experimental results can be distorted as they move from scientific journals into general discourse.

When we began tracing back the references to studies of EEGs on nine- to twelve-week-old fetuses, we found that they led to a conference that was held at the Charles University in Prague in 1968. Digging out the conference proceedings (no mean feat, we might add), we found that they referred back to a study done in Finland in 1963 and published in the *Annales Chirugiae et Gynaecologiae Fenniae* (Finnish Annals of Surgery and Gynecology). The original article, happily, was in English, so we were able to find out what had actually been done in the study.

For what were termed therapeutic reasons, Bergstrom and Bergstrom, the authors of the article (see the bibliography) had performed a series of Cesarean abortions at quite early stages of pregnancies, from 59 days (8½ weeks) to 158 days (22½ weeks). In this procedure, they removed the fetus from the uterus surgically. After they had carried out the procedure, and while the fetus was still alive, they inserted electrodes into three different regions of the brain and measured the voltage. These regions were the brain stem, the hypothalamus, and the top of the cortex. When the authors made their measurements, they found that there was, indeed, a time-varying electrical potential of a few microvolts (about one one-thousandth of the voltage across an individual axon membrane) from the electrode in the brain stem. In the older fetuses (from 84 days on), they occasionally saw electrical activity in the brain stem in response to touching the fetus in the region of the mouth. A few signals were recorded from the hypothalamus in the oldest fetuses, and no signals whatsoever were recorded from the cortex. These measurements, as far as we can tell, are the sole source of the claim that there is electrical activity in the brain of nine- to twelve-week-old fetuses.

Before analyzing the results, we should point out that it is inconceivable that an experiment of this type could be done in the United States today. We do, however, find it ironic that the results of the experiment, which treated the human fetus as an object of experimentation, form such a large part of the basis for right-to-life arguments (see below).

If you think about this experiment for a moment, you will realize that the mere presence of an electrical signal has nothing to do with normal brain activity. As we pointed out earlier, *every* cell exhibits some sort of electrical activity. If you placed electrodes on two sides of the cell membrane of a paramecium (as biologists often do these days), you'd also get a time-varying electrical signal. The fact that you get an electrical signal from cells just tells you they're alive. Indeed, the Finnish surgeons saw similar electrical activity when they stimulated the fetus's leg muscles.

The brain stem, you will recall, governs the most fundamental body functions: heartbeat, respiration, and automatic muscle responses. Every vertebrate, from a codfish to a Nobel laureate, has a functioning brain stem. The fact that electrical signals can be evoked in the brain stem by external stimulation just means that the circuits that carry signals to the cerebellum have been completed.

It is much more significant that no activity whatsoever was seen in the cortex, and almost none in the hypothalamus, even in fetuses well into the fifth month of development. What this means is that the Finnish experiment, far from disproving our argument about the development of the cortex, provides strong evidence for it.

Finally, we have to point out that none of the readings taken on the fetuses showed any trace of the kind of organized activity we associate with the EEG. In fact, most of the readings from the brain stem look very much like those taken from the muscle. They in no way indicate the presence of a being capable of sentient thought or even of sensation.

This simple fact has not, of course, prevented this particular canard from being repeated over and over in the abortion debate. This situation does, however, illustrate the importance of scientific honesty in the discussion of social issues.

A Word about "The Silent Scream"

One of the most influential films about the abortion debate has been "The Silent Scream." It portrays, in graphic terms, the reactions of the fetus during an abortion, and it invites the viewer to identify with it. The fetus in question was about twelve weeks old, and a sample of the movie soundtrack gives the message: "Now this little person at twelve weeks is a fully formed absolutely identifiable human being. He has had brain waves for at least six weeks . . ."

Let's look at this film in the light of what we have learned about the development of the fetus and, in particular, the development of the brain. At twelve weeks, the fetus has virtually no connections in its cerebral cortex. It is simply incapable of feeling emotions like fear. It is also incapable of moving in response to any willful thought. This statement has nothing to do with ideology; it follows from what we know about which parts of the brain control volition and when those parts of the brain start to function.

Thus the idea that the fetus can recognize the danger facing it from the abortionist's instrument and can try to escape is ridiculous on its face. It represents what philosophers call the *pathetic fallacy*. It is a result of our tendency to attribute emotions and motives to things that don't possess humanness. Walt Disney made a sizable fortune exploiting this tendency in his movies, but that's no reason to allow it to affect the outcome of the abortion debate.

The basic argument in the film, stripped of the emotional content of the soundtrack, is that the fact that the fetus can move makes it special. A similar argument (used often by medieval scholars) has often been applied to quickening, the time when a woman is aware of the motion of the fetus in her uterus.

We know, however, that there is no necessary connection between motion and mental awareness or conscious thought or volition. Here are some examples of phenomena that back up this statement:

• When a doctor wants to test your reflexes, he or she hits your knee with a little hammer to see if your leg moves. When the hammer hits the tendon in the knee, it stretches the muscles and causes a nerve impulse to travel from the nerve–muscle junction to the spinal cord. There the impulse is routed directly to the nerve that triggers the contraction of muscles in your leg, causing it to move. In this case, the movement takes place without any brain involvement at all (although in adults some signals do go on to the brain so that we are aware of the motion). The response is automatic, a fact that is recognized in our use of the term *knee jerk* to describe an unthinking reaction in political thought.

• Some animals are perfectly capable of motion even when decapitated. The phrase "running around like a chicken with its head cut off" arises from observation. One of the authors (JST) can remember visiting his grandfather and watching chickens being slaughtered. Occasionally one would get loose after its head had been cut off and would run around for an appreciable part of a minute, even though there were no signals going from the brain to the muscles. The existence of a brain simply isn't a necessary precondition of movement.

• Plants can move in response to stimuli, even though they don't have nerves. The Venus flytrap is one example; the mimosa, whose leaves fold up when they are touched, is another; the sunflower following the sun is a third.

Thus the fact that a fetus moves tells us nothing about the state of development of its brain. In particular, it tells us nothing about whether the synapses that give the brain its final configuration have formed. As far as the acquisition of humanness is concerned, the ability to move is simply irrelevant.

7

Survival Outside the Womb: Hitting the Wall

The original scientific basis for *Roe v. Wade* depended very little on fetal development per se. Instead, a great deal of emphasis was placed on the ability of physicians to keep a premature infant alive outside the uterus. The distinction between the first two trimesters, when a woman was held to have a fundamental right of choice, and the final trimester, when the state was held to have an interest in the outcome of the pregnancy, was based on the finding that the beginning of the third trimester marked the point at which there was a reasonable chance that a fetus could survive (with medical care) and grow to a normal birth weight.

Our experience has been that there is a general feeling that advances in medical technology in the treatment of premature infants—a field now called *neonatology*—has progressed to the point at which this old distinction is no longer valid, and that physicians are now able to intervene successfully at earlier and earlier stages in the pregnancy. When we look at the state of neonatology, however, we find a very different situation. It is true that there have been enormous advances in the field in the last twenty years. These advances, however, have been primarily in the ability to improve the chances of survival in good health of a third-trimester infant. There has not been a corresponding lowering of the age at which medical intervention can produce survival. In other words, the chances of an infant born at twenty-three weeks are not significantly better now than they were when the *Roe v. Wade* decision was first made. A study published in the *New England Journal of Medicine* (by Hack and Faneroff; see the bibliography) makes this point. The study covered 227 premature infants born between 1982 and 1988 at the University Hospitals of Cleveland and concluded:

> Thus, despite the tendency to perform more Cesarean sections and active resuscitations, no improvement in the survival of babies with lengths of gestation below 25 weeks or birth weight under 750 grams [about 1¼ pounds] was observed. The probability of survival is very poor if the length of gestation is less than 24 weeks or the birth weight less than 600 grams [1⅛ pounds].

This result was certainly not anticipated by physicians. One prominent neonatologist we talked to, for example, spoke of his field as "hitting the wall." As we shall see in a moment, the existence of the "wall" is related to fundamental developmental processes in the fetus, and scientists are not likely to breach it in the foreseeable future.

In strictly logical terms, survivability has nothing to do with the acquisition of humanness. They simply mark two different stages in the development of a fetus. Nevertheless, the notion of survivability plays such a crucial role in the public debate on abortion that it is important to understand the extent to which limits are placed on neonatal technology by processes that we do not understand and, in any case, probably cannot control.

We can begin by asking a simple question: What is the probability that a premature infant, provided with state-of-the-art medical care, will survive? There have been many studies bearing on this question, and we discuss two typical examples. One is a study of 141 infants at the University of North Carolina Medical School in Chapel Hill (data in Figures 13 and 14); the other is a study of 450 infants at the Royal Victoria Hospital in Montreal.

Both of these studies tell the same story. Up to twenty-four weeks, the probability of survival is either zero or extremely low. From that point on, however, it rises dramatically, reach-

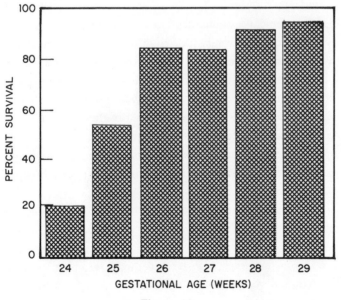

Figure 13

ing quite high levels by twenty-six weeks and staying there throughout the age range covered by the studies. For our purposes, the key point about the data presented in these studies is that a fetus has an appreciable chance of survival only after it has reached a gestational age of twenty-four weeks or, in the language of the abortion debate, has entered the third trimester.

At the lower age ranges, there is a difference in outcomes in the two studies. The probability of survival for a twenty-five-week fetus was significantly higher in the North Carolina study than in the Montreal study. This sort of thing is common in medical studies and has little significance for our argument. It is probably related to factors like differences in the techniques used at the two hospitals and differences in the sorts of populations served.

The sharp onset in survivability was what we referred to as "the wall." Without medical intervention, almost all of these infants would have died; a few of the older ones might have made it. The effect of intervention is to increase the survivability of infants in the twenty-four- to thirty-two-week group without, at the same time, having much effect on the survivability of the younger ones. Thus, the massive increase in medical capability has changed survival curves like these from ones that rose gradually to the present ones with sharp rise after onset of survivability as shown in Figure 14. In other words, there has not been a steady decline in the age at which survivability is first seen, nor is there any reason to argue, on either historical or physiological grounds, that there will be one in the near future.

The existence of the wall is shown even more strikingly in Figure 14, in which survivability is plotted in terms of the weight of the fetus at birth, rather than in time since conception. From this graph, we see that a fetus weighing less than five hundred grams (slightly more than one pound) has little chance of survival. Neonatologists usually talk about survivabil-

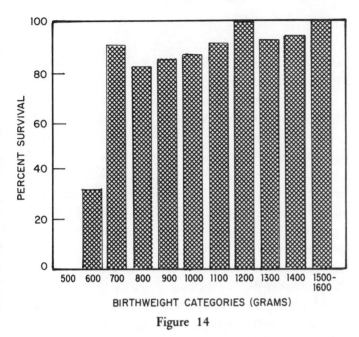

BIRTHWEIGHT CATEGORIES (GRAMS)

Figure 14

ity in terms of fetal weight, rather than age, because there are always uncertainties in determining the date of conception after the fact.

Why Is There a Wall?

A fetus removed from the womb before the third trimester faces a constellation of problems that, taken together, make it extremely unlikely that it will survive. All of these problems have to do with a point we made in Chapter 5: Fetal development is a process in which the gross outlines of organs appear quite early in the pregnancy, but the process of elaboration, of filling in the details, takes much longer. A premature birth, then, places extraordinary demands on organs that have not yet been completely formed, and that are therefore not up to handling the strain of functioning without the support provided by the uterus.

The most critical organs for our purposes are the lungs. They do not need to function *in utero,* of course, since the oxygen for the fetus is being supplied by the mother. The buds that will eventually develop into lungs appear during the fifth week, and the general structure (including the main bronchial tubes and the five lobes of the lung) can be seen at eight weeks. From then until the end of the sixth month, the tubes continue to branch; there are some seventeen generations of branching until birth and six more thereafter. The lungs of a child continue to develop during the first decade of life.

The working parts of the lung are called *alveoli* – small thin-walled sacs in intimate contact with capillaries. Carbon dioxide and other waste gases diffuse from the blood to the sac, and oxygen from the air we breathe diffuses in the other direction. Until about the twenty-fifth week, the sacs that will become alveoli have the character shown on the left in Figure 15. They are lined with thick-walled cells and are not in intimate contact with the capillaries. In this state, little diffusion can take place, and it is very difficult for the lungs to supply oxygen to the fetus.

Beginning at the end of the sixth month, the cells in the wall start to thin out and come into contact with the capillaries, as shown in the center of the figure. By the time of normal birth, the alveoli are fully developed, as shown on the right.

A second problem in lung development has to do with the presence of substances known as *surfactants* on the walls of the alveoli. The effect of these substances is to lower the surface tension at the blood–air interface. In premature infants, surfactants are not produced quickly enough to keep the surface

HISTOLOGICAL AND FUNCTIONAL DEVELOPMENT OF THE LUNG

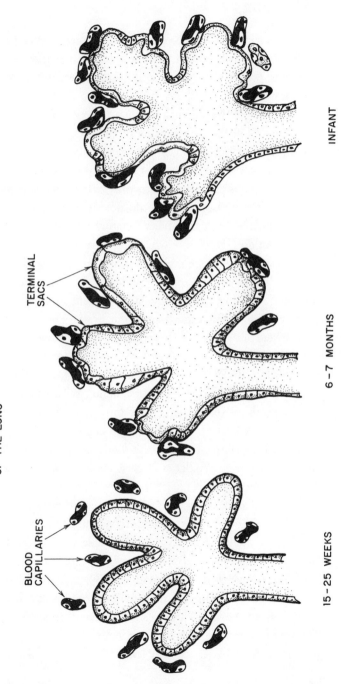

BLOOD CAPILLARIES

TERMINAL SACS

15 – 25 WEEKS

6 – 7 MONTHS

INFANT

Figure 15

tension down, and the alveoli collapse during exhalation and can't be reopened. Again, the production of surfactants increases as the fetus matures and is usually adequate in normal-term infants.

The point of this discussion of lung development is simple: If an infant's lungs are incapable of transferring oxygen from the air to the bloodstream, or can do so only inefficiently, the infant will not survive. The maturation of the alveoli, on the other hand, is a process that proceeds in the same way as the rest of fetal development. We do not understand these processes, much less have the ability to intervene and change them. All we can do is try to use what lung capacity there is to keep the infant alive until the maturation process is complete.

The second great group of problems faced by premature infants has to do with the circulatory system, and particularly with bleeding from capillaries in the brain. The situation is this: There are regions deep within the brain known as *ventricles*. They are small sacs whose function is to store spinal fluid. In the adult, the blood vessels that run through this region are supported and reinforced by surrounding cells. In the fetus, however, those surrounding cells form a kind of loose gel. They do not begin to provide a firm support until well into the seventh month of pregnancy. Under stress, this region of loosely supported capillaries is particularly prone to bleeding in premature infants.

In a premature infant, the failure of the lungs to oxygenate the blood means that the circulatory system has to work overtime to circulate what oxygen is available to the rest of the body. The capillaries in a region of the ventricles called the *germinal matrix* are thin-walled in any case, and when this extra strain is placed on them, they burst open, causing bleeding deep inside the brain. This so-called intraventricular bleeding is another major cause of death in neonates.

Another set of related problems arises because before the

beginning of the third trimester the skin is quite thin. When such an infant is exposed to air (in an incubator, for example), there is a great deal of water loss to evaporation. The infant quickly becomes seriously dehydrated.

The loss of water places a serious strain on the kidneys. You will recall (see page 88) that the details of the interior structure of the kidneys, as in the lungs, develop slowly as the fetus grows. One of the functions of the kidneys is to maintain the levels of salt in the blood. They do this by removing materials from the blood, then allowing only those materials that the blood needs to be reabsorbed. The unabsorbed materials are passed out as urine.

If salt concentrations in the blood are too high, the kidneys pull water from other parts of the body to dilute the blood and lower the concentrations. This is why drinking salt water makes one thirsty. In the neonate, the water loss through the skin raises the salt concentrations, and the kidneys are put under extra strain. Because the structure of the kidneys is not complete, they cannot meet the increased demand, and they fail.

The premature infant, then, faces a complex set of inter-related problems, all of which, ultimately, stem from the fact that crucial organs don't reach full operating potential until well into the third trimester. The sharp rise in the survivability data after twenty-five weeks attests to the skill of neonatal physicians in keeping infants alive once the lungs and the capillaries have reached minimum levels of development, and the low success rate before that time shows how futile it is to try to save an infant where they haven't developed enough.

Prospects for the Future

The question relevant to the abortion debate is whether or not the wall at twenty-five weeks will remain or whether new technologies will allow us to push it back. We feel that the existence of the wall is related to fundamental facts about human physiology, and that the present situation will persist into the foreseeable future. To see how we have come to this conclusion, ask yourself a simple question: What would it take to keep a twenty-week fetus alive until the lungs, capillaries, skin, and kidneys have developed to the point where the infant is past the wall?

At the minimum, the fetus would have to be put on some kind of machine that would oxygenate the blood and perform the dialysis normally done by the kidneys. Such a machine, if it existed, would have to remove blood from the infant's body, process it, and then return it. Physicians have accumulated a great deal of experience in the use of heart–lung machines on adults and children, as well as some information on implanting artificial hearts in adults. That experience indicates what to expect if we developed a lung–kidney machine for neonates. We can say with some certainty, then, that the basic problem would have to do with the formation of blood clots.

Blood is an extremely complex substance. It's not a simple fluid, like water, but a mixture of many different materials in a liquid matrix. Some authors go so far as to call it a *liquid tissue* to emphasize its complexity.

A little over half of blood is plasma, a yellowish liquid that contains many nutrients, hormones, antibodies, and other molecules. The rest is made of red blood cells (which carry oxygen to the cells), white blood cells (which attack foreign objects), and platelets. *Platelets* are products of cells in the bone marrow. When blood is exposed to air, or when it is subjected to strong forces, the platelets rupture and release chemicals into the blood. When these chemicals enter the blood, they induce a chemical reaction that produces a substance called *thrombin*. Thrombin, in turn, acts on proteins in the blood to form fibrin, a long, insoluble protein. The molecules of fibrin begin to lock together to form a mat (think of the fibrin molecules as strands in a bowl of spaghetti). This mat is what we see as a blood clot. To be complete, we should point out that clotting is actually a much more complex process than we've outlined here. Blood experts, for example, identified no fewer than thirteen clotting factors like thrombin in human blood.

Every heart–lung machine has to have a pump to move blood out of the body, through the system, and back into the body. It is a well-known problem that when blood is put through such a pump, the stress on the platelets (as well as the tendency of blood to clot when it encounters any nonbiological substance) is sufficient to trigger the clotting response outlined above. In fact, blood clots quite easily; when you have a blood sample taken, for example, the test tube has a little anticoagulant in it to prevent the blood from clotting because of its contact with the air. Heart attack patients are also given anticoagulants to prevent clotting as the blood moves around damaged tissue. In the body, blood is prevented from clotting by the anticoagulants manufactured in the capillary walls.

The same general technique is used in heart–lung machines. Drugs like heparin are injected into the bloodstream to inhibit the clotting response. It is usually possible to keep the level of anticoagulant low enough so that there are no serious side effects.

In our hypothetical lung–kidney machine for neonates, the same procedure would have to be followed. And that's where the problem arises, because, as we have pointed out, in neonates the capillaries in the germinal matrix of the brain aren't supported and have a tendency to bleed. If we add anticoagulants to the blood, we lower the ability of these capillaries to form clots to stop that bleeding. If we deal with one problem, in other words, we exacerbate the other. The simple physiological fact that both the lungs and the support matrix for capillaries are not functioning before twenty-five weeks means that there are almost insurmountable problems in increasing the survival rates for infants born before that time.

There is another point that should be made here, one that has not, to our knowledge, been emphasized in the abortion debate. The lung–intraventricular-bleeding problem is only the tip of the iceberg in the problems that would be encountered in trying to keep a second-trimester infant alive. If, against all expectations, some way could be found to get around the difficulties outlined above, we would then be up against the much more difficult (and more fundamental) problem of trying to supply the infant with all the materials it normally receives through the umbilical cord.

We know that the fetus receives both nutrients and oxygen from the mother. We also know that drugs and alcohol can come across the placenta as well. We have limited knowledge, however, about what else is exchanged between the fetus and the mother. There are surely hormones and other signaling molecules crossing the placenta in both directions, and it would be truly astonishing if this exchange didn't have an important effect on fetal development. At this stage, we know little about what hormones are involved, much less what effect they have.

It is reasonable to expect that the younger the fetus is, the more important will be its chemical interactions with its mother. It is very likely that keeping a second-trimester infant alive would involve a great deal more than simply supplying it with oxygen and keeping internal bleeding down. It would involve understanding and then reproducing the extremely complex biochemical interchange between the fetus and the mother. This task is well outside the capabilities of modern science, and it is likely to remain so for a long time.

It seems, then, that the current limits on survivability are likely to be a fixed feature of the abortion debate for the foreseeable future.

What about Early Survivors?

Despite the evidence of the survivability studies, the stories that stick in people's minds are the occasional remarkable survivals of extremely small infants; we've heard occasional anecdotal accounts of infants weighing less than five hundred grams surviving, for example. How can we square these spectacular cases with our arguments about the limits on survivability?

We will make three points. First, it is a simple matter of arithmetic that extremely unlikely events will happen if one waits long enough. The odds against having a coin flip come up heads ten times in a row is one in a thousand, for example, but if you do a thousand ten-flip trials, you are likely to get all heads in one of those trials. The *Guinness Book of World Records* is full of examples of improbable events that have happened, including one of a Russian pilot who survived a thirty-thousand-foot fall even though his parachute failed to open.

But the point about improbable events is that they are improbable. Most people who fall out of an airplane without a parachute will die when they hit the ground. Citing the record book doesn't change this fact. In just the same way, almost all babies born weighing under five hundred grams will not survive, and the fact that the rule is broken occasionally doesn't change the fact that it is a general rule.

More important, however, many of these seemingly miraculous survivals may not have involved infants of extremely low gestational age. To understand what we mean by this, you have to know what gestational age is and how it is calculated. On diagnosing pregnancy, the doctor asks a woman when her last period occurred. He or she then adds two weeks to this date and assigns that as the date of conception. That's when the gestational clock starts ticking.

This is really an imprecise way of dating conception, if for no other reason than the fact that women do not always keep a precise record of their menstrual periods. If the calculation isn't made until the second or third month of pregnancy (which is not uncommon), it is based on the woman's ability to recall the precise onset of a period that happened three months previously. How many of our women readers could date the beginning of the period they had three months ago? Add the fact that ovulation can occur anywhere from ten to seventeen days after the period starts, and you can see that there are large uncertainties in determining the gestational age.

The neonatal physicians we talked to suggested that the infant involved in the occasional story of very early survival was older than the official gestational age but, for some reason, was significantly smaller than average for that age. For example, one that was reported as surviving at twenty-two weeks might actually have been an undersized twenty-four-week infant. Given what we know about the problem of survivability, it's not hard to see why those two weeks would make a significant difference. A twenty-four-week infant, no matter how small, would have thin cells in its alveoli and a firmer support structure in its germinal matrix. Thus it would have a better shot at survival than its small size might suggest.

Finally, we should point out that there are some abnormal conditions—maternal heroin addiction, for example—that slow down the overall growth of a fetus but speed up the development of the lungs and other organs. Such infants, if premature, are likely to be assigned a young gestational age, but they have a reasonable chance of survival because their lungs and capillaries are ready for the strain.

Having said all this, we must discuss one further disagreeable fact. In the language of physicians, the term *survivability* means just that: the ability of the infant to remain alive. It says nothing about what we usually call the quality of life.

The fact is that the closer a premature infant is to the wall, the less likely it is to be healthy. Many 750-gram infants who survive turn out to have disabilities like severe cerebral dysfunction and mental retardation, and there seems to be no way of predicting the outcome of intensive-care procedures. This fact has led many in the field to question the usefulness of allocating scarce research funds to pushing survivability to earlier ages than those shown in Figure 14. The question that is asked is whether it is justified to expend limited medical resources in heroic efforts to keep extremely premature infants alive when there is such a need for those resources elsewhere. In the words of the authors of the study described above:

> Extremely low birth weight infants who require prolonged, often futile sojourns in neonatal intensive care units or who have poor longterm outcomes have become major consumers of health care resources and in some cases a major drain on health maintenance organizations. The allocation of limited resources may in the future mean denying care to some of these infants.

The Unexpected Coincidence

In Chapter 2, we saw that an accident of history has spared us from facing a difficult moral decision. The fact that Neanderthals and all of our other relatives are extinct means that we do not have to worry about the moral obligation we owe to beings that are very much like ourselves—beings with larger cerebral cortices than any other animals.

What we have discovered in this chapter is that we will not have to face another difficult moral problem. We know that significant numbers of synapses in the cerebral cortex start to connect during the seventh month of pregnancy. We have called this the period in which humanness is acquired. Now it appears that this period also coincides with the limits of survivability of newborns. In other words, it seems to be a general rule that *humanness and the ability to survive outside the womb develop at the same time*.

It may be that there are deep principles, as yet unknown, that require fetal development to proceed in this way, and it may be that there are not. If there are not, then we can imagine that the alveoli in the lungs could have been programmed to develop in the fifth month. If this had happened to be the case, then the major cause of death in very premature infants would be eliminated and the survivability curve in Figure 14 would cut off at twenty weeks instead of twenty-four without any change in the rate of cortical development. In this case we would have to grapple with the issue of what to do during the period when an infant could survive outside the womb and the period when it acquires humanness. If survivability and humanness were separated, we would have to decide whether abortions would be permissible during this period.

This would be a difficult problem indeed, for there would no longer be the conflict between the interests of the mother and those of the fetus. The fetus could be removed from the womb, and this removal would satisfy the woman's right to control her own body, but the fetus could be kept alive. One can only imagine the sorts of debates that would go on if this were the case.

The onset of survivability is related to the fundamental laws of fetal development. So is the acquisition of humanness. The fact that these two events occur at the same time allows us to use the concept of humanness in the abortion debate without having to worry about future complications due to advances in medical technology.

CHAPTER

8

Conclusions

Where have we come after our excursions into the varied corners of the scientific enterprise in the previous chapters? We have learned a great deal about fetal development, the limits of medical technology, and other subjects relevant to the abortion debate. In the end, however, all of this knowledge must be applied, and as we pointed out at the beginning, this means that our argument has to go outside the bounds of conventional science. Science describes what is, but we have now come to the point where we need to use this knowledge in making decisions.

Decisions cannot be made on purely scientific grounds. We can, however, use scientific information to guide our moral and political judgments. No matter which side of the debate we take in any public dispute, we should, at a minimum, get the facts straight and understand the scientific dimensions of the problem.

With these caveats in mind, we now turn to the body of

knowledge we have been exploring and discuss the policy implications that follow from, and are consistent with, the basic biology of reproduction.

Summary

We started our discussion by noting that *Homo sapiens* is both part of the web of life on our planet and yet distinct from it. Whether we start by looking at other forms of life that exist today or trace the development of our species through time, we see that what distinguishes human beings from other forms of life, both structurally and functionally, is the existence of a large, multiply connected cerebral cortex. In our usage, we say that our species acquired humanness when the enlarged cortex developed, and the individual human fetus acquires humanness when the cortex begins to function.

This conclusion led us to an examination of fetal development, where we found that the development of the brain follows a well-defined pattern. Up to the end of the second trimester of pregnancy, nerve cells accumulate in the brain and differentiate, but it isn't until the seventh month and beyond that significant numbers of connections between those cells are formed. Just as a pile of microchips isn't a computer, we argued, a pile of nerve cells is not a functioning cortex. It is only when the system is "wired up" by synaptic connections that the fetus, in our terms, has acquired humanness. This process starts at around twenty-four weeks of gestation and continues well into childhood.

In a turn of events that is, as far as we can tell at present, a coincidence, the period corresponding to the acquisition of humanness is the same as that at which a premature infant has a reasonable chance of surviving outside the uterus. Although medical technology has made great strides over the past several decades in improving both the chances of survival and the health of premature infants, there has been virtually no change in our ability to keep alive the infants born before twenty-four weeks. One neonatologist referred to this period as the "wall," beyond which we are unlikely to be able to move any time in the foreseeable future. The existence of the wall has to do with the maturation of the fetal lungs: until twenty-four weeks, they simply are not up to the task of supplying the body with oxygen. In addition, kidney and skin functions are not sufficiently developed to support external existence.

From a strictly logical point of view, this coincidence has no bearing on the question of humanness and abortion. Nevertheless, viability carries great weight with many people. As a matter of fact, one of the authors (JST) decided to participate in writing this book after a neonatologist friend pointed this coincidence out to him.

The existence of the coincidence means that we do not have to face the difficult questions that would arise if we could keep infants alive until their cerebral connections were made, or if we had to stand by and watch while a premature infant with a functioning brain died because it couldn't get oxygen into its bloodstream.

Recommendations

At the start of this book, we set out a general argument to establish the connection between abortion and the onset of humanness. As we pointed out, this particular connection is not based on scientific arguments and is therefore different in character from other parts of our presentation.

There is an abortion controversy because of a basic conflict between rights.* Whatever right a woman has to control the use of her own body must be balanced against whatever right to live is assigned to the fetus at a given stage of development. When the woman wishes to have an abortion, both rights cannot be exercised.

To us, it seems obvious that if a conflict arises between two beings, one of which has acquired humanness and the other of which has not, the rights of the former must take precedence. On the other hand, when the conflict arises between two beings that have acquired humanness, the state has a legitimate interest in the outcome.

We therefore propose the following guidelines for policies on abortion. These guidelines are consistent with (and influenced by) what we know about the development of fetal life:

1. Until the burst of synapse formation in the cortex during the seventh month of pregnancy, the right of the woman to choose must take precedence. During this period, abortion should be a matter of choice.

2. In the third trimester, mechanisms for decisions should take account of the concerns of the mother, the values of the community, and the realization that the fetus is acquiring a more and more fully functional cortex as time passes.

By tying the question of abortion rights to the onset of humanness, we feel that we have formulated a policy that is profoundly in tune with biological reality. The onset of humanness provides a fundamental (though at present imprecise) marker in the development of the individual, one that is differ-

---

*Throughout this chapter we will use the term *rights* in the colloquial, rather than the legal sense. Establishing the fetus's right to life or the woman's right to choice in the legal sense is, of course, what the abortion controversy is all about.

ent from either conception or birth. It should be accorded the importance it deserves.

Are These Recommendations Workable?

Given the way that synapses in the brain form, it is impossible to point to one instant in time and say, "Here's where the fetus has a fully functioning cortex." It's like trying to say at what point an opening door is open. The period of significant synapse formation that starts in the twenty-fourth week is a gray area, a time when decisions must be made on individual cases one at a time.

What happens at the beginning of the third trimester is not, then, the acquisition of humanness, but the loss of certainty. Before this time, we can present convincing arguments that the fetus has not acquired humanness. Once the burst of synapse formation starts, however, this denial is no longer possible. We can't say humanness *has* been acquired, but we can't say that it *hasn't*, either. This is a classical example of a gray area.

Making decisions in a gray area is difficult, but we have found ways to make them in other cases. In our view, a decision on a third-trimester abortion is similar in some ways to the decision to withdraw life support systems from a comatose patient. In both cases, there is a sense of the seriousness of the decision: a great deal is at stake. In both cases, the decision is seen to be difficult, and in both cases, it is seen to be too important to be left solely to a single individual without rules and guidelines.

In the case of terminating life support, a system has evolved in which, in most cases, hospitals and physicians respond to professional and public regulations. Occasionally, however, there are cases in which the guidelines are not clear, and in these cases hospital ethics boards, including physicians, religious leaders, and lay citizens, wrestle with the decision. In this system, the values of the community can be brought to bear on specific cases.

Could a similar system be used to deal with third-trimester abortions? This depends on how many such abortions there are, since it would be difficult to make decisions on a case-by-case basis if this number were to be very large.

As it happens, the number of third-trimester abortions in the United States is hard to determine exactly. The Centers for Disease Control compiles abortion statistics from 36 states, and finds that approximately 1 percent of abortions occur after the twenty-first week of gestation. If this statistic applied nationwide, there would be about 10,000 abortions annually in this period. In this data set, all abortions at or after twenty-one weeks are lumped together.

How many of these 10,000 occur after our cutoff of twenty-four weeks? If we simply extrapolate the CDC data, we find that the number is too small to be determined accurately. The number is estimated to be as low as 100 abortions annually in the pro-choice literature, and we can find nothing in the CDC data to contradict this estimate. We can conclude, therefore, that no single hospital would have to deal with more than a handful of cases each year. This would hardly be a strain on the system.

The Theological Tradition

Although we have arrived at our empirical conclusions strictly on the basis of scientific reasoning, we should point out that they resonate with one strain of thought in twentieth-century Roman Catholic theology. As we indicated earlier, a number of theologians have, quite independently, come to the conclusion that the cerebral cortex is the defining mark of the human being, the thing that sets us apart (at least in the material sense) from other animals.

This line of thought springs from a problem that all theologians faced at the end of the nineteenth century. If one accepts Darwin's idea (as biologists have) that human beings descended from the same ancestors as all other animals, how, then, can one make humans special in the sight of God?

One man who thought deeply about this problem was the French Jesuit priest Pierre Tielhard de Chardin. He was a theologian, of course, but he was also a paleontologist of some note in the early part of this century. To a man with this particular mix of intellectual interests, the prospect of finding a way to reconcile his church's teachings with what had become an accepted description of the natural world must have been very attractive indeed. In the end, he came to regard the development of the enlarged cerebral cortex as almost a second creation—as a sign from God that humanity is, indeed, special, regardless of the fact that we share a common ancestry with all other life. This notion has echoed through the twentieth century and, as we have pointed out, still characterizes a strain of Jesuit thought today.

Having said this, we should hasten to add that Roman Catholic theologians who might agree with our basic scientific views would not necessarily agree with our suggestion of how these views ought to be applied in the abortion debate. Nonetheless, their having traveled down at least part of this road gives some support to our arguments.

Does the Fetus Suffer?

In the early nineteenth century, the English social philosopher Jeremy Bentham introduced an important change into discussions of ethics in the context of the debate over the proper treatment of animals. He argued that whether or not an animal had a soul was irrelevant; what mattered was whether the animal experienced pain and suffering. This notion has become deeply ingrained in our thinking. It is the basis for our current laws regarding the proper treatment of animals.

It also has an obvious role to play in the abortion debate. Regardless of whether the fetus has a functioning cortex, its suffering pain during the abortion process would make a difference in the way we approach the issue. Indeed, the entire thrust of the film "The Silent Scream" was to try to convince the viewer that the fetus was being put to a particularly gruesome and painful death. This claim is misleading at best and fraudulent at worst.

Insofar as this issue is important in the debate, it provides added bolstering to our designation of the onset of humanness as the crucial point in the pregnancy, for the fact of the matter is that before the wiring up of the cortex, the fetus is simply incapable of feeling anything, including pain.

Look at it this way: On any day of the week, open heart surgery is being performed at hospitals all around the country. In this operation, an incision is made in the chest, the sternum (breastbone) is split, and then a device not very different from a car jack is used to spread the ribs apart so that the surgical team has access to the heart. It is literally impossible to imagine the level of pain the patient would feel were he or she not under anesthetic. Yet if you talk to people who have had the operation, you find that they remember nothing of it; they went to sleep before it started, woke up after it was over, and felt nothing in between.

While the surgery is in progress, nerves in the body are sending signals to the brain; the more intense the pain, the greater the frequency of the pulses on the nerve axons. The anesthetic, by a process still imperfectly understood, prevents the brain from receiving these signals and interpreting them as pain. The result: The patient feels nothing and remembers nothing even though the nerves are sending out impulses.

We would argue that before the onset of humanness, the fetus is protected by the best anesthetic imaginable. The signals may be sent by the nerves, but there is simply nothing to receive them. They stop at the brain stem for the simple reason that there is nowhere else for them to go. The fetus feels no pain for the simple reason that it can't feel anything.

An analogy may help make this point. Right now, the room where you are sitting is flooded with signals from radio and TV stations. They're all around you, even passing through your body. Yet unless you turn on your radio or TV, you remain unaware of their presence. As far as you are concerned they might as well not be there at all.

For the fetus, the onset of humanness is like the turning on of the radio. Until then, it makes no difference how many signals are being sent by the nervous system; nothing can be felt, and the fetus simply cannot suffer in the sense that we (and Bentham) use that term.

Once the synapses start forming, however, this sort of categorical statement can no longer be made. We don't yet know enough about how the brain processes signals to be able to say which synapses have to be in place for the fetus to feel pain. This is another example of how one loses certainty after the onset of humanness.

Roe v. Wade

Our proposals are similar to those set forth by Justice Blackmun in the *Roe v. Wade* decision. This similarity wasn't intentional, but neither is it accidental. The scientific input into that decision had to do primarily with survivability, and the third-trimester cutoff on the right to unlimited abortion was based on the fact that in 1973 that seemed to be the point at which the fetus could survive outside the womb. At the time, there was a good deal of criticism based on the notion that medical science would keep pushing this limit down, necessitating frequent recourse to the courts in the future.

Few people in 1973 anticipated the existence of the wall, or the fact that the third trimester represents a fundamental limit on survivability. Thus, what was seen as a kind of temporary stopping point on the road to ever-increasing technological ability in neonatology has turned out to be, in a very real sense, the end of the road. At this level, the fact that our recommendations coincide with the argument in *Roe v. Wade* is just a reflection of the fact that physicians had already approached this fundamental limit in 1973.

The abortion legislation in the foreseeable future is likely to revolve around questions that have nothing to do with the issues we've raised in this book. For example, knowing about the onset of humanness provides no guidance whatsoever on questions such as whether the parents of a pregnant teenager must be notified of an abortion or must give their consent to it.

This is not to say that the sciences have nothing to say about abortion, of course, but simply to stress the point we made at the very beginning of our discussion. Abortion is an issue that involves many questions, and science can answer only some of them. As informed citizens, we have views on these other sorts of questions, of course. It's just that our background as scientists gives us no special insights into them. Our personal views are just that: personal views. On these topics they carry no more weight than those of any other citizen.

Afterword

In the first seven chapters of this book we have tried to present basic science and the conclusions that follow from it as objectively and impartially as we can. In Chapter 8 we have presented the policy implications that, in our view, follow from our definition of humanness as related to fetal development.

No one comes to the question of abortion without preconceptions. Everyone has an opinion on the controversy; indeed, the authors have never had so many intense, emotionally charged discussions with people as they did during the writing of this book. Although we do not think that our presentation hinges critically on our personal views, we nevertheless feel that we should make these views known to our readers.

We were rather surprised to discover that, although we had only minor disagreements while sifting through the body of scientific work that makes up most of this book, we were not able to agree on a single statement of personal views at the end.

Harold Morowitz

Formulating the abortion issue in terms of humanness allows one to make rational distinctions between a microscopic fertilized ovum and a newborn infant. These distinctions permit a discussion of abortion in less personal, emotional terms and shift the debate to more public and less burdened concepts. In this context, the emergence of social personhood as distinct from an anatomical and physiological existence is better defined and made more explicit.

Because the onset of humanness is quite discrete, it is possible to assign a period (the first two trimesters) during which a woman's choice is the sole determinative in abortion. This period accords with the *Roe v. Wade* decision because viability, on which that decision was based, coincides with the onset of humanness. At some time during the third trimester, when humanness has emerged, the state acquires an interest in the developing fetus. This interest is usually exercised in the licensure and regulation of physicians and the chartering and regulation of hospitals.

Third-trimester abortions usually involve crises and anticipated catastrophes. It is clearly in the best interests of everyone involved that these decisions be made with a maximum of compassion, a minimum of bureaucratic interference, and the absence of attorneys.

James Trefil

When I started working on this book, I felt that there was an absolute and inviolable right to choice on the woman's part. Had I been pushed, I suppose I would have argued that this right held until the moment of birth. This view arose from a background of traditional Jeffersonian conservatism – the feeling that the government simply has no business telling people what to do. I had always been concerned that people who called themselves conservatives were so willing to interfere in the lives of others.

The effect of sifting through the scientific literature, then, has been to move me both toward a less absolute position and to make me realize that after the onset of humanness, the interests of the fetus must be taken into account along with those of the woman.

Having said this, I should add that I don't think that abortion is ever a good thing. It is only the least bad of the available choices. I sympathize completely with people I talked to who are repelled by the notion of teenage girls using abortion as a means of birth control, and I agree that the best solution would be a system in which situations like that never arise.

In an ideal world, in fact, there would be no abortion debate. Every child would be wanted; every fetus would be surrounded by a constellation of adults waiting joyously to nourish it and bring it to a happy adulthood. There would be no conflict of rights, because every pregnant woman would have chosen to use her body to produce a child.

But we don't live in an ideal world. Conception can (and does) occur as a result of rape and incest. It occurs because people are careless, and it occurs because, even when they're careful, no method of birth control is perfect. It does no good to tell someone, "You should have been more careful," even if it's true, because you are still faced with the question of what to do about the pregnancy.

In the end, the abortion controversy comes down to one question: Will *this* particular pregnancy be terminated or not? There are only two possible choices, neither good. One is to abort the fetus. The other is to demand that the pregnancy be brought to term and, in effect, to compel the birth of an unwanted child.

The second choice is repugnant to me. Not only does it entail real and immediate risks for the mother, but it may create a lifetime of misery for the child—misery that will, in all likelihood, persist for generations. Frankly, I can imagine fewer human acts more deeply evil than bringing an unwanted child into the world.

Bibliography

1. Asking the Right Question

Doerr, E., and Prescott, J. W. 1990. *Abortion Rights and Fetal "Person-hood."* Long Beach, CA: Centerline Press.

Dubos, R. 1968. *So Human an Animal.* New York: Scribner's.

Goldenring, J. M. 1985. The Brain-Life Theory: Toward a Consistent Biological Definition of Humanness. *Journal of Medical Ethics* 11:198.

Gray, G. W. 1948. The Great Ravelled Knot. *Scientific American* 179 (Oct.):26.

Hall, E. 1989. Does Life Begin? *Psychology Today* (Sept.):43.

Jones, D. G. 1989. Brain Birth and Personal Identity. *Journal of Medical Ethics* 15:173.

Macphail, E. M. 1982. *Brain and Intelligence in Vertebrates.* London: Oxford University Press.

Oppenheimer, J. M. 1967. *Essays in the History of Embryology and Biology.* Cambridge: MIT Press.

2. The Web of Life

Dutta, S. K., and Winter, W. P. 1990. *DNA Systematics*. Boca Raton, FL: CRC Press.

Purves, W. K., and Orians, G. H. 1983. *Life: The Science of Biology*. Sunderland, MA: Sinauer Associates.

Voet, D., and Voet, J. G. 1990. *Biochemistry*. New York: Wiley.

3. The Biology of Conception

Kaufman, M. H. 1983. *Early Mammalian Development: Parthenogenic Studies*. Cambridge, England: Cambridge University Press.

Solter, D. 1988. Differential Imprinting and the Expression of Maternal and Paternal Genomes. *Annual Review of Genetics 22*:127.

4. The Emergence of Humanness

Carter, G. S. 1967. *Structure and Habit in Vertebrate Evolution*. Seattle: University of Washington Press.

Dodson, E. O. 1960. *Evolution: Process and Product*. New York: Reinhold.

Farb, P. 1978. *Human Kind*. Boston: Houghton Mifflin.

Fenster, E. J., and Sorhannus, R. 1991. On the Measurement of Morphological Rates of Evolution: A Review. *Evolutionary Biology 25*:375.

Gould, S. J. 1977. *Ontogeny and Phylogeny*. Cambridge: Harvard University Press.

Grant, V. 1977. *Organisms and Evolution*. New York: W. H. Freeman.

Johanson, D., and Shreeve, J. 1989. *Lucy's Child*. New York: Morrow.

Leakey, R. E., and Lewin, R. 1977. *Origins*. London: Macdonald and Janes.

Loomis, W. F. 1988. *Four Billion Years: An Essay on the Evolution of Genes and Organisms*. Sunderland, MA: Sinauer Associates.

Mayr, E. 1976. *Evolution and the Diversity of Life*. Cambridge: Harvard University Press.

5. The Development of the Fetus

Benirschke, K. 1967. *Comparative Aspects of Reproductive Failure*. New York: Springer-Verlag.

Gilchrist, F. G. 1968. *A Survey of Embryology*. New York: McGraw-Hill.

Glees, P. 1988. *The Human Brain*. Cambridge, England: Cambridge University Press.

Häring, B. 1972. *Medical Ethics*. Slough, U.K.: St. Paul Publications.

Lenihan, John. 1975. *Human Engineering*. New York: Braziller.

Nelsen, O. E. 1953. *Comparative Embryology of the Vertebrates*. Toronto: Blakiston.

Noden, D. M., and DeLahunta, A. 1985. *The Embryology of Domestic Animals*. Baltimore: Williams & Wilkins.

Sadler, T. W. 1985. *Langinan's Medical Embryology*. Baltimore: Williams & Wilkins.

Steven, D. H. (Ed.). 1975. *Comparative Placentation*. London: Academic Press.

Tanner, J. M. 1978. *Fetus into Man: Physical Growth from Conception to Maturity*. Cambridge: Harvard University Press.

Teilhard de Chardin, P. 1959. *The Phenomenon of Man*. New York: Harper & Row.

Thompson, R. F. 1975. *Introduction to Physiological Psychology*. New York: Harper & Row.

Wendell-Smith, C. P., Williams, P. L., and Treadgold, S. 1984. *Basic Human Embryology*. Mansfield, MA: Pitman.

6. The Birth of the Cortex

Bergstrom, R. M., and Bergstrom, L. 1963. Prenatal Development of Stretch Reflex Functions and Brain Stem Activity in the

Human. *Annales Chirurgiae et Gynaecologiae Fenniae*, Supplement 117.

Bindman, L., and Lippold, O. 1981. *The Neurophysiology of the Cerebral Cortex*. Austin: University of Texas Press.

Brazier, M. A. B., and Petsche, H. (Eds.). 1978. *Architechtonics of the Cerebral Cortex*. New York: Raven Press.

Desmedt, J. E. (Ed.). 1977. *Visual Cortical Potentials in Man: New Developments*. London: Oxford University Press.

Engel, R., and Butler, B. V. 1963. Appraisal of Conceptual Age of Newborn Infants by Electroencephalographic Methods. *Journal of Pediatrics 63*:386.

Glees, P. 1988. *The Human Brain*. Cambridge: Cambridge University Press.

Goldenring, J. M. 1985. The Brain-Life Theory: Toward a Consistent Biological Definition of Humanness. *Journal of Medical Ethics 11*:198.

Klemm, W. R. 1969. *Animal Electroencephalography*. New York: Academic Press.

Llinas, R. R. 1990. *The Workings of the Brain: Development, Memory, and Perception*. New York: W. H. Freeman.

Low, H. O. C. 1982. *Developmental Neurology*. New York: Raven Press.

Moore: K. L. 1988. *The Developing Human: Clinically Oriented Embryology*. Philadelphia: W. B. Saunders.

Purpura, D. P. 1975. Morphogenesis of the Visual Cortex in the Preterm Infant. In M. A. Brazier (Ed.), *Growth and Development of the Brain*. New York: Raven Press.

Rakic, P., Bourgeois, J., Eckenhoff, M., Zecevic, N., and Goldman-Rakic, P. 1986. Concurrent Overproduction of Synapses in Diverse Regions of the Primate Cerebral Cortex. *Science 232*:232.

Scott, D. 1976. *Understanding the EEG: An Introduction to Electroencephalography*. Philadelphia: Lippincott.

Sidman, R. L., and Rakic, P. 1982. Development of the Human Central Nervous System. In W. Haymaker and R. D. Adams (Eds.), *Histology and Histolopathology of the Nervous System*. Springfield, IL: Charles C Thomas.

Thompson, R. F. 1975. *Introduction to Physiological Psychology*. New York: Harper & Row.

7. Survival Outside the Womb: Hitting the Wall

Avery, G. B. (Ed.). 1987. *Neonatology*. Philadelphia: Lippincott.

Bergstrom, R. M. 1986. Development of EEG and Unit Electrical Activity of the Brain during Ontogeny. In L. J. Jilek and T. Stanislaw (Eds.), *Ontogenesis of the Brain*. Prague: University of Karlova Press.

Collins, J. 1992. Calf Extract Benefits Premature Infants. *National Center for Research Resources Reporter 16*:6.

Hack, M., and Faneroff, A. A. 1989. Outcome of Extremely Low Birth Weight Infants between 1982 and 1989. *New England Journal of Medicine 327*:1642.

Hellegers, A. 1978. Fetal Development. In T. Beauchamp and L. Walters (Eds.), *Contemporary Issues in Bioethics*. Evanston, IL: Dickerson.

Holmes, G. L. 1986. Morphological and Physiological Maturation of the Brain in the Neonate and Young Child. *Journal of Clinical Neurophysiology 3*:209.

Rosenthal, E. 1991. As More Tiny Infants Live, Choices and Burden Grow. *New York Times* (Sept. 29), p. 1.

Wood, C., Katz, V., Bose, C., Goolsby, R., and Kraybill, E. 1989. Survival and Morbidity of Extremely Premature Infants Based on Obstetric Assessment of Gestational Age. *Obstetrics and Gynecology 74*:889.

Young, E. W. D., and Stevenson, D. K. 1990. Limiting Treatment for Extremely Premature Low Birth Weight Infants (500–750 g). *American Journal of Diseases of Children 144*:549.

8. Conclusions

Doerr, E., and Prescott, J. W. 1990. *Abortion Rights and Fetal Personhood*. Long Beach, CA: Centerline Press.

Dunstan, G. R. 1984. The Moral Status of the Human Embryo: A Tradition Recalled. *Journal of Medical Ethics* 1:38.

Gordon, M. 1990. *Good Boys and Dead Girls*. New York: Viking.

Grobstein, C. 1988. *Science and the Unborn: Choosing Human Futures*. New York: Basic Books.

Hackerman, N. 1988. *Use of Laboratory Animals in Biomedical and Behavioral Research*. Washington: National Academy Press.

Lederberg, J. 1967. The Legal Start of Life. *Washington Post* (July 1), p. 50.

Teilhard de Chardin, P. 1955. *The Phenomenon of Man*. New York: Harper & Row.

Tribe, L. H. 1990. *Abortion: The Clash of Absolutes*. New York: W. W. Norton.

Index